Getting GRAMMAR

150 New Ways to Teach an Old Subject

Donna Hooker Topping

Sandra Josephs Hoffman

HEINEMANN Portsmouth, NH

Heinemann
A division of Reed Elsevier Inc.
361 Hanover Street
Portsmouth, NH 03801–3912
www.heinemann.com

Offices and agents throughout the world

Library of Congress Cataloging-in-Publication Data
Topping, Donna.
    Getting grammar : 150 new ways to teach an old subject / Donna Hooker Topping and Sandra Josephs Hoffman.
        p. cm.
    Includes bibliographical references.
    ISBN 0-325-00943-0 (alk. paper)
    1. English language—Grammar. 2. English language—Grammar—Study and teaching.
I. Hoffman, Sandra Josephs.   II. Title.
    PE1112.T67 2006
    428.2′071—dc22   2006006025

Editor: Kate Montgomery
Developmental editor: Kerry Herlihy
Production editor: Sonja S. Chapman
Cover and interior design: Jenny Jensen Greenleaf
Compositor: Publishers' Design and Production Services, Inc.
Manufacturing: Steve Bernier

Printed in the United States of America on acid-free paper
10 09 08 07 06 VP 1 2 3 4 5

In memory of
James Hooker, Rabbi Louis Josephs, and Dora Wolf Josephs.
They would be so proud.

Contents

Foreword

How many times have you cringed when spotting grammatical or usage errors on signs, menus, billboards or advertisements?

In *Getting Grammar*, authors Donna Hooker Topping and Sandra Josephs Hoffman, turn these mundane mistakes into classroom conversations by asking students to photograph and create a collage of their discoveries. Likewise, such surprising texts as knock jokes, nursery rhymes and newspaper headlines become grist for the grammar mill, as Donna and Sandy share myriad ways to joyfully study parts of speech, correct usage, syntactic elements, and common errors.

Yes, *Getting Grammar* is a book chock full of inviting ways to share grammar information with students. But it is so much more.

It is a book that reminds educators that all instruction should be assessment-driven. The authors wrote this book in response to the felt needs of the student teachers in their university classrooms, many of whom were asked to teach grammar in their student-teaching assignments.

It is a book that offers educators historical background on the teaching of grammar, encouraging educators to not be afraid of controversial topics and compelling readers to ask themselves, "Where do I stand on the grammar wars?"

It is a book that encourages educators to maintain their role as decision-makers, asking themselves, "Which of these classroom activities make sense for my students, in my school, in my district?"

It is a book that helps educators support English Language Learners and helps them understand the grammatical misunderstandings of these students. After all, in Japanese, the typical word order is subject-object-verb. In Farsi, adjectives follow nouns, verbs are at the end of the sentence, and pronouns are omitted if they are understood. In Spanish, verbs indicate tense and number.

It is a book that reminds educators what Grammar 101 was all about, complete with definitions of terms. Are your students' writing folders filled with a rich array of declarative, interrogative, imperative, and exclamatory sentences? Can you spot dangling participles and misplaced modifiers?

It is a book that gives educators permission to carve out time for good old-fashioned fun and games amid all those ever-growing, somber, and serious assignments and assessments. When was the last time your students played *MadLibs*, Charades, or Musical Chairs?

It is a book that reminds educators to keep up with children's literature, studding each chapter with ample bibliographies and offering many ways to delight in the grammatical constructions of favorite authors. Audrey Wood's *The Napping House* has tantalizing verbs. Lewis Carroll's *Jabberwocky* has intriguing sentence constructions. Judith Viorst's *Alexander and the Terrible, Horrible, No-Good, Very Bad Day* clearly illustrates how strings of adjectives can be used for emphasis.

It is a book that demonstrates how to weave content studies into the Language Arts arena, learning content and grammar through crossword puzzles, riddles and even by playing Truth or Dare.

It is a book that honors the arts in education, demonstrating how grammatical elements can be taught through art, movement, music, and drama. Have you ever thought to study the preponderance of pronouns in patriotic songs?

It is a book that fills readers with surprising facts. *The House that Jack Built* is modeled after a sixteenth-century Hebrew chant. *Over the River and through the Wood* was written by one of the earliest American women to make a living as a writer. Irregular verbs used to be called strong verbs and regular verbs were known as weak ones.

Getting Grammar is also a book with big ideas running through it, ideas that run through many student-centered reading and writing workshops. Throughout, the authors remind us that. . . .

Decision-making must rest with those whose practice will be affected by those decisions.

Description of teaching practice is different from *pre*scription of practice.

The teaching of grammar should be part of a program that is rich in reading and writing.

Put authentic writing and reading ahead of everything else.

Read aloud to students every single day.

Share your own writing with your students.

Build student's ownership and joy about their language through real reading and writing, through dramatics, art, and music.

Take your cues from your students' writing and from their curiosities about language.

No doubt, readers of this book will discover ways to engage students in grammar study, become motivated to invent their own unique ways to do likewise, become self-conscious about their own grammar and usage demons, and most of all be inspired to ask at their next faculty meeting, "So what do we think about the study of grammar?"

—Shelley Harwayne
March, 2006

Acknowledgments

Our students at Millersville University are the next generation of teachers, and they give us great hope for the future. Already, they are steeped in the habit of reflective teaching. Not only do they reflect on what they know and don't know, but they actively seek to fill any gaps they have. Truly, it was they who led us to this book. We are grateful to all of them, particularly to Brian Bogart and Katie Jones, who were the first to look us in the eye and tell us we needed to do more with grammar. These students have watched the development of this book, eager for every detail of our writerly lives. They helped us hone our skills as we developed theirs.

Several of our students—Jenine Melo, Erin Squibb, Renee Buchanan, Jessica Kennedy, Erin Freneaux, Na Park, Jamie Witmer, Marlania Collins, Dagny Heidig, and Kerianne Kotsur—graciously posed for the pictures found in this book. We thank them for being good sports. Our graduate assistants, Kristi Klunk and Katie Holland, were masters at keeping track of details and helping out in so many ways. We are so fortunate to be surrounded by all of these teachers of tomorrow.

We are grateful to the wonderful folks at Heinemann. Editors Kate Montgomery and Kerry Herlihy gave us the most insightful comments on our manuscript and never ceased to cheer us on. Sonja Chapman and Doria Turner masterfully shepherded us through the production process. Working with them has been our pleasure, and writing for Heinemann has been an honor.

Our friends and professional colleagues Pat Wendell, Teresa Pica, Roberta McManus, and Jean Bender were never more than a phone call or an email away when we had questions or needed help. We thank them for being there.

Finally, we so appreciate our devoted families. Kathryne Hooker, Donna's real mother and Sandy's "adopted" mother, supported us with love and pride throughout every step of developing this manuscript. Donna's children, Allyson and Ed Stallman and Brad Topping, answered all of our technology questions and brought levity to even the most intense writing sessions. Sandy's daughter Sharon and son, David, both accomplished writers, willingly shared their expertise. Her daughter Alisa, son-in-law Dan, and granddaughters, Dori and Kate, provided long-distance encouragement and enthusiasm throughout the process. And, as always, Sandy's husband, Jerry, provided regular and continual support. We thank all of them for being in our lives, for navigating the cascading piles of manuscripts in our homes, and for enduring our constant grammatical corrections!

Important, Yet Playful, Grammar

If . . .

you engage your students in lots of writing,

you immerse your students in reading lots of authentic children's literature,

you think you should teach something about grammar but are not certain of your own grammar knowledge,

you know that you should use your students' writing to teach minilessons on grammar, but you need some extra ideas,

you are looking for ways to teach grammar that are different from the boring ways in which you remember being taught,

you believe that language exploration, of which grammar and usage are part, should be playful,

. . . then

this just may be the book for you.

■ Why This Book Came About

We are professors of literacy education who teach undergraduate elementary teachers-to-be about the teaching of literacy. Brian, one of our teacher-education students, set off for his first meeting with his field experience cooperating teacher. She told him that he was going to be teaching a unit on grammar, verbs in particular. He panicked. "I sat in front of my computer staring at the screen as I attempted to write out a unit plan. *How*, I thought, am I going to make this interesting and real to these third graders?"

We find that Brian's experience is not unusual. More and more of our students are being asked to teach grammar during their field experiences. We also find that they clutch. Many of them never were taught grammar and usage directly, having gone through school when direct instruction in grammar and usage was not in vogue. Others have a vague memory of it being taught, but not much more than that. Still others have disturbing memories of having to slog through endless memorization drills and worksheets. Many of them feel like Katie, another of our teachers-to-be, who confided her fears on the eve of her field experience: "Please, oh please, don't let my cooperating teacher ask me to teach a unit on grammar!"

Our students' experiences set us off on an exploration. We developed a survey and sent it to twenty school districts that lie within the service area of our university to determine if and how grammar is included in the elementary school curriculum. Concurrently, we surveyed our teacher-education students about their recollections of being taught various aspects of literacy, including grammar and usage. The results confirmed what we had been sensing. The schools into which our students were going were teaching grammar, and our students did not feel prepared for the task.

We realized that we needed to do something to help our students fill in their gaps. We needed a down and dirty review of grammar and usage to make sure they had the content knowledge they needed. However, the idea of assigning a basic grammar book or developing one of our own did not resonate well with us. Our minds kept returning to Dan Lortie's (1975) findings about what influences how teachers teach. He found, simply put, that they rely on their apprenticeships of experience (the way they have been taught) and observation (the way they have seen teachers teach). We knew from surveys of our students that those who remembered being taught grammar and usage were operating from apprenticeships of worksheets and drill. The thought of providing them with a review that would simply become a template for drills and worksheets frightened us. We realized that we needed to provide an intervention, one that would give our teachers-to-be a collection of strategies to teach grammar and usage in ways that were lively and active—ways in which they likely had not been taught.

In their field placements, our students often are asked to conduct *Daily Oral Language K–12* (1993), a daily drill in editorial correctness. To familiarize them with this drill, we decided to begin each class with our own version of *Daily Oral Language*. We made it our own by rechristening it "Help! Editor Needed!" and then expanded it into a quick drill for the identification of the parts of speech and parts of sentences as well. We were inspired by our students' enthusiasm for this relatively painless look at language and then broadened their focus to the world outside of the university classroom. We challenged them to photograph environmental print in which they found errors in grammar or usage. Their excitement for this task was matched only by their outrage at the sloppiness they found on signs and announcements in public places. Their collections quickly turned into a large bulletin board (see Figure 1–1) at the university and portfolios for their future classrooms. In class, we shared the creative ways in which Brian, our once-panicking student, turned the dullness of grammar into a lively art. And before long, this book began to form in our minds . . . .

FIG. 1–1 *Help! Editor Needed! bulletin board*

■ A Brief History of the Grammar Wars

Conversation about grammar is not new. Over the years, as with many aspects of literacy instruction, educators have disagreed about the importance of teaching grammar formally. Until quite recently, a number of educators agreed that grammar should not be taught directly. Many of our students, in fact, seem to have been caught in this trend when they were in school—a worrisome thing for us, in that they now are becoming the teachers who are charged with teaching it. But, the pendulum appears to be swinging once again, this time sweeping a more holistic look at grammar in its arc, as the following brief history will tell.

Charles Fries (1952) is credited with an early anti–grammar instruction position. A renowned linguist, he set the stage for the foremost professional organization for English teachers, the National Council of Teachers of English (NCTE), and its national following to discourage the teaching of grammar. In an NCTE report officially titled Research in Written Composition, Braddock, Lloyd-Jones, and Schoer (1963) led the antigrammar camp by stating that teaching formal grammar did not improve students' writing and might even have a deleterious effect upon it. As recently as 1991, NCTE reaffirmed its position about the negative effect of teaching grammar (Hillocks and Smith 1991). Although NCTE maintains its opposition to the formal teaching of grammar, a small special-interest group called the Assembly for the Teaching of English Grammar (ATEG) has grown from within NCTE's ranks, and NCTE published Brock Haussamen's *Grammar Alive!* in 2003. Clearly, there is opposition to the antigrammar stance, albeit tiny.

Recently there has been a plethora of articles and books on the subject of grammar, and the argument goes on. While some researchers confirm the antigrammar stance, others speak out in support of formal grammar instruction. In *The War Against Grammar* (2003), David Mulroy offers such a case. He introduces the reader to various elementary schools in the United States that teach grammar directly in their literacy curricula. Constance Weaver (1996) takes the middle road when she states that grammar instruction should be embedded in a subject. She suggests that we teach "a minimum of grammar for maximum benefits" and writes of the need for a "scope-not-sequence" chart of concepts that should be taught some time between kindergarten and graduate school (16). Her chart includes aspects of grammar that are most important to writers:

> ▶ teaching concepts of subject, verb, sentence, clause, phrase, and related concepts of editing,
> ▶ teaching style through sentence combining and sentence generating,
> ▶ teaching sentence sense and style through the manipulation of syntactic elements, and
> ▶ teaching the power of dialects and dialects of power (16–17).

In practice, many teachers continue to adopt, and adapt to, a more middle ground. In his article "Correct Grammar So Essential to Effective Writing Can Be Taught—Really!" (1996), Alvin Brown describes how he teaches traditional grammar and punctuation and gives the reader hints about doing the same, debunking common misconceptions about grammar. In "Integrated Word Study: Spelling, Grammar, and Meaning in the Language Arts Classroom," Invernizzi, Abouzeid, and Bloodgood (1997) propose incorporating instruction in grammar into a broad word study plan in the upper elementary school grades. Hunter (1996), another grammar proponent, has developed his own program as a result of his research. Sams (2003) underscores the belief that grammar and writing are linked together, inseparable from one another. Martinsen (2000) offers further moderation in stating, "It [grammar] should be neither abandoned nor worshipped but appropriately placed within the discipline of English" (125).

Debates and polarization in the teaching of grammar continue in the theoretical world, but as we can see, practitioners are not purists. Some study their own practices and do what is right for their particular students. Others are guided by externally imposed curricula or national trends such as the new Scholastic Aptitude Test. Still others, we suspect, are simply not sure what to do.

■ Where We Stand on Grammar and Usage

The time has come for us to declare our stances on the subject. Underlying what we write herein are several beliefs that stand as the basis for our work on this subject.

Over our multidecade careers as educators, we have become more and more convinced that the critical questions and answers in education must be posed and researched by the teachers and administrators who are affected by them. This requires that they come to terms with their own belief systems, those systems that direct them from the shadows of their minds. We have found that, all too often, educators willingly abdicate their rights and responsibilities to make decisions, using the protective shield of "But so-and-so [the latest guru] says that it's best to . . ." Our work over the years (Hoffman and Topping 1999, 2000; Topping and McManus 2002b; Topping and Hoffman 2003) consistently has advocated that only those *within* a school or district can know what is best for their particular context. Those outside of this context can hold valuable opinions and can offer the findings from their own contexts as worthy food for thought, but the ultimate right and responsibility for decision making rests with those whose practice will be affected by the decision. In short, teachers and administrators must be researchers of their own school-based practices. Especially in the grammar-and-usage debate, relying upon so-and-so to direct what a school or district should do is dicey, at best, because many different so-and-sos say divergent things on this subject. We repeat: Teachers and administrators need to make their own informed decisions. This is ever so important when there is not consensus in the field.

BELIEF 2 *There Is a Place for the Teaching of Grammar in Our Practice*

Based upon our own research on our teaching, we have come to believe that grammar, indeed, needs to be taught. Our fledgling teachers are being asked to teach it. We know that they, like speakers and users of any language, have *tacit* grammar in their heads. What they need is a metalinguistic awareness of it. They need *to know about what they know* about the language to be able to step outside of themselves and explain it to their students in a meaningful way.

Our belief in the need to teach grammar, however, goes further than our responsibility for preparing teachers. The study of grammar gives us terminology to use when we talk about improving writing. Without terminology, discussions of writing would simply skirt around the edges. We would say things like, "Your something-or-other and your something-or-other, you know . . . like . . . don't agree," or "You need to put in some more words that tell about it," or "You have two something-or-others here separated by a comma," when it would be so much more economical to say, "Your subject and verb do not agree," "You need a stronger verb," or "You have a comma splice here."

While having shared grammatical terminology makes it easier to talk about writing, knowledge of grammar, in itself, does not improve writing. As a matter of fact, studies over the years have consistently shown that the teaching of grammar does not automatically improve writing. Conversely, teaching writing does not automatically improve one's knowledge of grammar. Writing is writing. Grammar is grammar. They are related and symbiotic in nature, but neither necessarily is causal of the other. A robust program in reading and writing provides context into which the study of grammar becomes richer. But grammar is a body of knowledge unto itself, a vehicle for sound learned expression that fully literate people need to have.

BELIEF 3 *Knowledge of Grammar Is Important in a Multilingual Society*

In an increasingly more global and multilingual society, becoming facile with the grammar of new languages will be difficult without an operating knowledge of the grammar of one's native language. Today's children will become adults in a world that will require them to speak instantly and comfortably with others from around the world and within their own society. How will they be able to learn the subtleties of the syntax of other languages without names for features of their own? Consider, for example, Haussamen's summary of the ways in which other languages differ from English:

1. The nouns might take gender.

2. Other languages may use articles differently or no articles at all.

3. Plurals may be formed by adding words or syllables to the sentence, or by giving context clues in the sentence to indicate that there is more than one of something.

4. The word order may not follow the familiar subject-verb-object pattern.

5. The pronoun may not have to agree in gender or number with its antecedent.

6. Other languages may have fewer prepositions, making it confusing for the novice to know which preposition to use in English. Also, the preposition may not precede its object.

7. There are differences in inflection and pacing.

8. There are differences in written conventions, such as punctuation and capitalization.

9. Nonverbal communications, such as gestures, eye contact, silences, and what people do to indicate that they understand, differ from culture to culture (2003, 55).

It seems a tall order to expect our future citizens to come to terms (no pun intended) with the descriptors of a second or third language when they don't know the terms that describe their first language.

BELIEF 4 *Description Is Different From Prescription*

While we are treating you as mature users of the language and will be *describing* language, we don't *prescribe* that you teach it as a set of rules, even though that's the way you may have been taught. We feel that, too often, the linguistic description of the grammar of our language has, de facto, served as the prescription for teaching it. You know the drill: *A noun is the name of a person, place or thing. Repeat after me, . . .*

a noun is the name of a person, place, or thing. Now, take out your worksheets and underline the nouns. Not only is this boring, but it's quite abstract. As a matter of fact, it's four abstractions away from the real thing. Think about it. We have a concrete item that exists in space—a chair, for example. Then we have the mental recognition of the chair. Then we have a word for that mental construct, the word *chair*. Finally, we have the word *noun* that describes the word *chair*. Grasping this is no small task for a young student.

BELIEF 5 *Put Authentic Writing and Reading First— in the Middle—and Last*

The teaching of grammar should be part of a program that is rich in reading and writing. In the past, the problem was that the teaching of grammar and usage often absorbed all of the time that might (and should) have been spent engaging children in reading and writing. Writing and reading the works of other writers provide a rich context for the study of language. Without that context, isolated study of grammar and usage is a detached and futile exercise. It is within the context of *our own words* and the words of *authors we love* that caring about grammar can happen.

Read Aloud Every Day

So much that constitutes proper usage comes more from an ear that has heard language used well than from a brain that has processed a set of caveats. It pains us when we hear talk of abandoning read-aloud to make time for direct instruction that meets state standards. Clearly, we have no problem with minilessons that focus on the parts of language—that's what this book includes—but not when they occur to the exclusion of the real processes of literacy in action. As you, a literate adult, read through the descriptions of language we have included in this book, you undoubtedly will be comparing what we say with your own tacit knowledge of grammar. That tacit understanding comes from your lifetime of immersion in language as a whole—from hearing it, reading it, writing it. Without these in situ experiences, you would have difficulty connecting with what we've written. Children deserve the same. *Read to them every single day.* Let them hear language used well. Let them bask in its radiance. Give them the same advantage you have had as a fully literate person. If a decree banning read-aloud has descended upon your school, close your door and read aloud anyway.

Share Your Writing

Share your writing with your students. Keep a journal, write poetry, write letters to the plumber who overcharged you or to an elderly aunt in another state, a to-do list, a quick note reminding yourself to pick up the dry cleaning, or that children's book that has been in your mind for years, and let your students see you as an author. Let them see you as a writer who sometimes struggles with proper usage and who savors reading that writing over when it's the way you want it. Let them know that you consult references. Let them see you as a human being who constantly is learning and using language.

We both share the writing that we do with our students—the writing that has been published, the writing that hasn't been published, the writing that is part of our lives. We show them manuscripts. The hundreds of pages that we wrote before the two-hundred-page book or the ten-page article became final. We show them the mess. We share the comments that editors have made about our writing. We marvel at how feedback from others helped us know what we had to say. We also are always amazed at how alert our students become when they hear an author talk. It is these authorial moments that provide the context for grammar and usage.

BELIEF 6 It's Not a Question of Whether to Teach Grammar, But How

By now, you know that we believe that the teaching of grammar and usage is important. But, more importantly, we believe that the study of grammar and usage should be playful. It should engage children's *multiple* intelligences (Gardner 1993) in order to draw them into the learning. Fortunately, our teacher candidate Brian was a creative person. He found ways of incorporating creative dramatics into the mundane life of singular and plural verbs. His students laughed as they acted out verbs in class and on the playground. They came to own verbs in their own special way. He took a topic that traditionally has been taught in a left-brained manner, one involving the linguistic intelligence only, and made it accessible for his students. And that is our point in this book. We advocate bringing grammar to life in ways that are playful, inclusive, and exciting. We want to build children's ownership of and joy in their language—through real reading and writing, through the dramatics, art, and music.

But I *Loved* Grammar!

Before we go on, let us recognize those among us who loved the isolated study of grammar, who thought that diagramming sentences was close to an act of worship, and who aced every one of those grammar-in-isolation tests. Perhaps those among us were working from strong logical/mathematical and linguistic intelligences. To be sure, those are two very important ways in which people are smart. But, if Gardner (1993) is correct, there are five others—spatial, musical, bodily/kinesthetic, interpersonal, and intrapersonal. We wonder how many more of us might have been invited into the study of grammar and usage if all of the human intelligences had been activated. In an educational system meant for all people, wouldn't this be a more inclusive and democratic way of teaching and learning? This is what we suggest in this book. Art, music, movement, and drama—bring on the arts in the study of grammar and usage!

So, Where Do You Stand on the Issue of Grammar?

You know how we feel. We can only share our findings based on our context. So, go ahead. Ask yourself why you are (or are not) teaching grammar. If the answer is "Because it's in (not in) the curriculum," the anonymous "*They* say I have to (or shouldn't)," or "So-and-so says . . . ," that's not good enough! Stop right now. You and your colleagues need to examine your beliefs about this. Should you or shouldn't you? If, after a lot of reading, thinking, observing, and talking, the answer is "Yes, we should," then read on. Perhaps you will be able to use some of the ideas that have worked for us on our turf. We encourage you to share your feedback and other active strategies for teaching grammar and usage with us.

You may be wondering what to do when. Our advice is that you take your cues from your children's writing and their curiosities about language. What shared terminology do you need in order to talk with them about their writing? What kinds of words and structures in their writing could you use as springboards to some of the minilessons in this book? What rich language do the authors of your shared reading texts use that you could build upon? Although there is no universal agreement about what to teach when, we have included a summary of what schools in our area report that they do in Appendix A. You may find that it gives you a general direction in terms of what commonly gets taught in what grade. Once again, however, this decision belongs to you and your colleagues, based upon your informed conversations.

■ What to Expect in the Rest of This Book

We have tried to design this book to be reader-friendly. Now that Chapter 1 has given you a window into our minds, here is what you can expect. Chapters 2 through 7 present an overview of sentences and the parts of speech. In each, we begin with a brief review. Next, we present ideas for minilessons that are playful and make grammar come alive. We have identified the type of each activity with an icon.

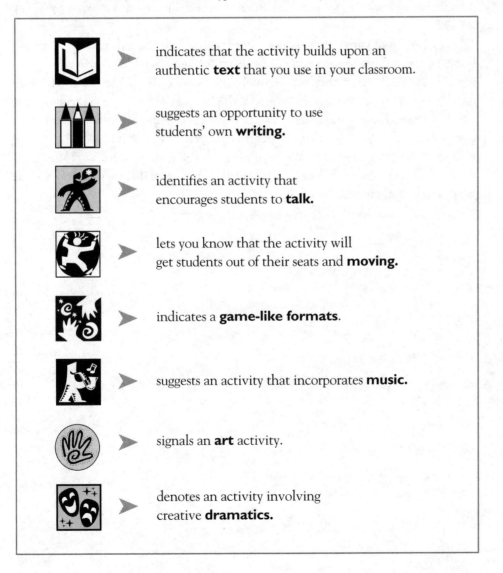

indicates that the activity builds upon an authentic **text** that you use in your classroom.

suggests an opportunity to use students' own **writing.**

identifies an activity that encourages students to **talk.**

lets you know that the activity will get students out of their seats and **moving.**

indicates a **game-like formats**.

suggests an activity that incorporates **music.**

signals an **art** activity.

denotes an activity involving creative **dramatics.**

Because we know that your students may come from many other first-language backgrounds, we include a sampling of information about how sentences and parts of speech are regarded in different languages. We were staggered to learn that there are thousands of languages spoken in the world. Young speakers of these languages enter American classrooms and, all too often, are labeled as *deficient* or *disabled* when they are not. They simply bring their first-language grammar to the study of English, grammar that may or may not be a match for the way English works. Many American teachers speak only English and are not aware of the structure of other languages, so we offer this section not as a comprehensive linguistics course or an overview of all languages, but a heads-up about language differences that may appear in your children's writing.

Each chapter ends with "Check It Out!"—an opportunity for you to test your own knowledge of the grammar content presented therein. The passages used are pieces written by children in the fourth through eighth grades, followed by questions that ask you to identify parts of speech in their writing.

In Appendix B, you will find a comprehensive self-test that covers all of the content of the book—another way for you to check up on your own understanding of the grammar of English language speakers. Appendixes C, D, and E will provide you with still more resources for your classroom. Appendix F contains answers to Check It Out!

So, whether you are relatively new to this thing called teaching, like Brian and Katie, or you are a seasoned veteran in search of ideas, enjoy! We have not reinvented the wheel here; rather, we have delved into our own work and the rich works of colleagues past and present to bring you the best of the best. If you regularly provide the context of writing and reading of beautiful children's literature, we have a treat for you. This book is playful. It treats language in a way that causes kids to love it, savor it, long for more of it. Will you use all of the ideas in this book? We doubt it, unless you have more days in your school year than most do. So, pick and choose, adopt and adapt, but most of all, have fun!

Sensible Sentences and Categories of Clauses

Sentences and clauses are the meat and potatoes of the grammar meal. If authors don't understand the basic structure of a sentence, they won't get their meaning across to the reader. Although the staples of subject and verb are essential, there is much more for students to learn (and teachers to teach). Writers who are able to season these basics by using different sentence types—declarative, interrogative, imperative, and exclamatory—are well on their way to spicing up the repast. But let's not stop there! Dependent and independent clauses are like the side dishes that add interest to a meal. When authors vary their sentence lengths by using simple, complex, compound, and compound-complex sentences, they tantalize the reader's tastebuds and invite him to stay for the whole meal. All told, sentences and clauses make writing palatable, interesting, and—dare we say it?—they can be great fun to teach!

You may be thinking, Declarative, interrogative, and exclamatory sentences. Which is which? Complete subjects and predicates. Is a predicate the same as a verb? Independent and dependent clauses. Independent or dependent of what? And don't even mention simple, complex, compound, and compound-complex sentences to me! If I am this overwhelmed, how will my students feel? How will I make this comprehensible for them? Take a deep breath because a brief review and a menu of activities follow.

Quick Review for Teachers

Basic Parts of a Complete Sentence

Subject (who or what) Ex. *The grateful student*
　　Simple Subject: usually one noun or pronoun. Ex. *student*
　　Complete Subject: simple subject with all its modifiers. Ex. *The grateful student*

Predicate (action) Ex. *thanked the teacher for the grade*
　　Verb: action or being. Ex. *thanked*
　　Complete Predicate: verb and all its modifiers
　　　　Ex. *thanked the teacher for the grade*

Types of Sentences

Declarative: makes a statement; ends with a period.
  Ex. The computer crashed last night.

Interrogative: asks a question; ends with a question mark.
  Ex. When did the computer crash?

Imperative: states a command or strong request; ends with a period or exclamation point. *Ex. Fix the computer now.*

Exclamatory: expresses strong emotion; ends with exclamation point.
  Ex. This is such a mess!

Clauses Within Sentences

Independent Clause: can stand alone as a complete thought.
  Ex. You will get good grades

Dependent Clause: needs more to complete the thought. *Ex. If you study hard*

Simple Sentence: has one independent clause. *Ex. He enjoyed the rigor of school.*

Complex Sentence: has one dependent and one independent clause.
  Ex. Although he had many hardships, he enjoyed the rigor of school.

Compound Sentence: has two independent clauses joined by a conjunction or a semicolon. *Ex. He had many hardships, but he enjoyed the rigor of school.*

Compound-Complex Sentence: has two independent clauses and one or more dependent clauses.
  Ex. Although he had many hardships, he enjoyed the rigor of school and he loved to talk about learning.

(Goldstein, Waugh, and Linsky 2004, 77–83; Brandon 2006, 27–30)

■ Playing with Sentences and Clauses

Serve Your Sentence

Many of us remember playing truth-or-dare as children. Our friends asked us questions and we had to answer them truthfully or do whatever they dared us to do. Serve Your Sentence is a modification of this game, without the dare part. On three slips of paper, each student writes a declarative sentence telling a classmate to do something, an interrogative sentence asking a question, and an exclamatory sentence that a classmate has to act out. On the reverse side of each slip of paper the author writes whether the sentence is declarative, interrogative, or exclamatory. Collect these and place them in a container labeled "Serve Your Sentence." One by one, students come to the front of the room and draw a slip of paper, announce the kind of sentence, and respond appropriately to what their sentence indicates. Of course, you will remind them that school language and school rules apply to what they write.

Materials needed: three-by-five-inch cards or slips of paper, pencils, container

Share the Wealth

Forget those isolated practice exercises! Inside every piece of writing—your students' and that of the beloved authors whose works you share—is a wealth of possibilities for sentence work. Ask students to take out a piece of writing from their folders. Then have them underline or highlight the aspect of sentence structure you are studying—a declarative sentence, a compound sentence, a dependent clause, or subject and predicate. They can use different highlighters for different types of sentences or parts of sentences. For variation, have students use a class text or independent reading book and identify these features. Use this as a quick assessment to check for understanding.

Materials needed: current texts, students' writing, highlighters

High Fives for Complete Sentences

Using any current text, read aloud either complete sentences or fragments. (For the fragments, simply read part of a sentence.) In pairs, students slap a high five (slap each other's hands over their heads) when they hear a complete sentence and cross their arms across their chests when they hear a fragment. Of course, they are allowed to confer with each other before making their moves, so use a signal of some sort (a bell or a verbal cue) to give them time to review with each other before acting.

Materials needed: current texts

Content Area Riddles

This activity will give you an opportunity to review content area material while practicing types of sentences. Linguistically, what is a riddle but two or more declarative sentences followed by an interrogative sentence? Chances are, your students never have thought of it this way, but they probably are quite familiar with the format of a riddle. For example, *I am the seventh planet from the sun. My atmosphere would not support human life. I have rings made from gases. Who am I?* Write the riddle formula on the board: declarative sentence + declarative sentence + declarative sentence + interrogative sentence. Challenge them to follow this format to create riddles about a current unit of study. Share these and enjoy a quick content review at the same time.

Materials needed: riddle formula on board, paper and pencils

The Traveling Tale

In the typical traveling tale, students each write an opening sentence and then pass the tale to a second student, who adds a second sentence before passing it to a third student, and so on. In this variation, each student pulls a kind of sentence (declarative sentence, complex sentence, exclamation, simple sentence, or whatever you have been studying) from a bowl. This is the kind of sentence they will write in the traveling tales that they start and continue to tell. Before they begin, make sure to offer to review what constitutes each sentence type so everyone is prepared. At your signal, they each write the opening sentence of a tale. When you sense that all are ready, signal for them to pass their tale to the next student, who reads what has been written and then adds the next sentence in the story. Partway through, you can have students pass their sentence type to the next student, as well, so they get to practice with more than one kind. When interest seems to be waning, stop the traveling and ask for volunteers to read their tales aloud.

Materials needed: slips of paper, container, paper and pencils

Roberta's Circles

Roberta McManus (Topping and McManus 2002b) first used Circles as a review activity in science, but it is applicable to any content. Draw three large circles on the board and label one as "Complete Subjects," the second as "Complete Verbs," and the third as "Complete Objects." Using review sentences from your content area, write the subjects of these sentences in the "Subjects" circle, the verbs in the "Verbs" circle, and the objects in the "Objects" circle. Have students choose one word or phrase from each circle to combine into an accurate sentence, both in content and grammar. They can write the sentence on sentence strips to share with the class. This idea is easy to vary. Students can make up their own review sentences, break them apart into circles on paper, and trade with each other to check for accuracy. You also can write review sentences on sentence strips, cut them apart into individual words, and draw circles on the board labeled "Simple Subjects," "Simple Verbs," and "Simple Objects." Add a fourth circle labeled "Miscellaneous Words" into which you place the other parts of speech (see Figure 2–1).

Materials needed: sentences from content area text, chalkboard and chalk, sentence strips, marker, pencils

Five About Food

Your students may come from different places and speak multiple languages, but they all have favorite foods. Invite them to each bring in an empty container that formerly held one of their favorite foods—a candy bar wrapper, fast-food container, or a soda can, for example. Their task is to write five complete sentences about this food, underlining the subject once and the predicate twice in each. This use of environmental print will provide an impetus for talking and comparing among students with similar food preferences but different language backgrounds. Partners with sim-

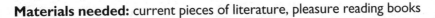

FIG. 2–1   *Roberta's circles*

ilar food tastes can collaborate on their sentences, making this a perfect scaffolding activity for nonnative English speakers.

Materials needed: food wrappers and packaging, paper and pencils

Nonsentence Sense

If you examine well-written prose, you'll notice that authors use complete sentences more often than not. Periodically, though, they use sentence fragments that just seem to resonate with their voices. In fact, they use them purposefully—for emphasis, to show exhaustion, to create rhythm, and for a host of reasons that match the overall context of what they are writing. Help your students analyze these choices, and they will become more sophisticated readers and writers. Using a current piece of literature, highlight a passage that includes traditionally complete sentences as well as a fragment or two. Model your thinking about the kinds of sentences the author has written and help students brainstorm a list of reasons they think he has chosen to use the fragment. What effect did he want to have on his readers? How well does it work? Have students do the same with their current pleasure reading books and share their discoveries with the class. Encourage them to use this type of structure in their own writing. Robert Burleigh's *Home Run* (1998) is one great example. Think about his use of sentence fragments to punctuate a point: "Then it is as it should be. Smooth as silk. Easy as air on the face. Right as falling water" (n.p.).

Materials needed: current pieces of literature, pleasure reading books

Walking in Authors' Footsteps: Sentences

Katie Wood Ray's *Wondrous Words* (1999) is a treasure of ways to get young authors to learn to write by studying the craft of other writers. By examining how published authors construct and vary sentences, you can provide footprints in which your developing writers can walk. Ray suggests two texts that present a great opportunity to talk about sentences. In *Welcome to the Green House* (1993), Jane Yolen creates an almost musical pattern with the following trio of sentences:

> Welcome to the green house. Welcome to the hot house. Welcome to the land of the warm, wet days. (n.p.)

Cynthia Rylant uses a run-on sentence very effectively to rush the reader through a long time period of anticipation in *The Relatives Came* (1985a):

> So they drank up all their pop and ate up all their crackers and traveled up all those miles until they finally pulled into our yard. (n.p.)

While these two excerpts are good examples, there are many more in the beloved texts that you use. As a teacher, begin to "read like a writer" (Ray 1999, 12), always alert to beautiful ways in which writers vary sentence length and break traditional rules about things like run-ons. Point these out to your students. Your conversation might sound like this: "Let's look at this sentence in [name of book and page]. Listen and follow along while I read it. [Read it aloud.] I just think it's beautiful because it makes me feel/sounds like/gives me the sense that . . . Why do you think [author] wrote it this way? What kind of sentence is it? How and why does it work?" Encourage your students to *read like writers*, too. Invite them to locate five sentences in their current pleasure reading book that are particularly interesting and effective. Have them copy them onto a paper, identify each type of sentence, and highlight the clauses. Encourage them to share their findings with a partner, hypothesize about what the author did, and then write their observations about this author's sentence use at the bottom of the page. Have them post these observations in an authors' corner for all to see.

Materials needed: authentic texts, pleasure reading books, paper and pencils

Who Wrote These Titles, and Why?

As part of reading instruction, teachers typically call students' attention to textbook access features such as chapter titles, headings, subheadings, and captions. They tell them that authors and editors add these elements to make the text clearer to the reader. We suggest taking this one step further, playing with the grammatical patterns contained within them. Invite students to identify the types of structures the authors and editors decided to use, and to speculate on why they used them. Ask questions like, "What kinds of sentence or clause structures did this author use in her titles, headings, subheadings, and captions? Why do you think so? In what other ways could she have written them? How could we turn the title of Chapter 2 into a simple sentence?" Engage your students in discussing and rewriting these signposts. Not only will you reinforce grammar, but you'll help them focus their reading, as well.

Materials needed: current textbooks, nonfiction trade books, paper and pencils

Let's Make the Test

Make a deal with your class: you will let them help construct the upcoming grammar test on sentences and clauses. Have them each choose example sentences and clauses from their writing folders, or their pleasure reading books, for each of the categories that will be on the test. Tell them you will include at least one example from each person on the test. As students submit these to you in writing, you will see rather quickly who does and does not understand, and you'll be able to do some one-to-one teaching ("Alisa, I'm not sure this really is a compound sentence. Let's look at the clauses . . . ."). This makes a nice formative assessment before the "big one."

Materials needed: paper and pencils, writing folders, pleasure reading texts

Yellow and Green Clauses

Place two pieces of construction paper, one yellow and one green, on the board. On the yellow piece, write, "Dependent Clause. Caution! Not complete!" On the green piece, write, "Independent Clause. Go! Complete!" Give each student two smaller pieces of construction paper, one yellow and one green, and have them label them like the ones on the board. Now you are ready for an activity in which every student will respond individually. Slowly read aloud phrases you have identified in one of their current texts. If students hear a dependent clause, they hold up the yellow paper. If they hear an independent clause, they hold up the green paper. In a glance, you will be able to see who understands, who hesitates, and who doesn't get it at all.

Materials needed: yellow and green construction paper, one piece of each for each student, plus two to display, current texts, marker, pencils

Coloring my Clauses

Have students take a draft from their writing folders and color lightly over their clauses—yellow for dependent and green for independent. Once their drafts are color coded, they will be able to count how many simple, complex, compound, and compound-complex sentences they have used. Not enough variety? Have them work with a partner to try combining or separating clauses into new sentence forms.

Materials needed: crayons or colored pencils, drafts of writing

The Strangest Magazine We Ever Read

Collect old magazines until you have enough to provide one for each student. Give them each ten minutes to cut out complete sentences from their magazine. (Captions

and large-font introductions work well because they are larger.) Have students then cut their sentences into subjects and predicates, placing each in a pile on their desk. Working in pairs, students combine their two piles of subjects and two piles of predicates. Drawing one subject and predicate at a time, they combine them into new sentences and glue them onto a piece of construction paper labeled "The Strangest Magazine We Ever Read."

Materials needed: old magazines, scissors, construction paper, glue, markers

Reconnect

Lift complex and compound-complex sentences from the book you are reading aloud to the class. Break them into their dependent and independent clauses and write these clauses on sentence strips. Give a sentence strip to each student, then have students walk around the room until they find the rest of their sentence. Don't be surprised if there are some reconnects that are different from the original sentences but that make sense nonetheless!

Materials needed: current read-aloud book, sentence strips, markers

Clause Pause

Clause Pause is adaptable to any board game. Ahead of time, prepare cards on which you write independent clauses (on about two-thirds of them) and dependent clauses (on about one-third of them). Any of the books you use in your classroom would be good sources for these. Before students take their turn in a game, they must draw a card. If they draw an independent clause, they can move forward in the game. If they draw a dependent clause, they must skip their turn.

Materials needed: three-by-five-inch cards, markers, class texts, board game of choice

Artistic Clauses

Brainstorm with your class to identify a list of possible motifs that would capture the essence of dependent clauses and independent clauses. (For example, dependent clauses might be represented by a baby, independent clauses by a parent; dependent by a seed, independent by a flower.) Encourage creativity and outside-the-box thinking. Have pairs of students decide which motif they prefer, draw and cut out an $8\frac{1}{2}$-by-11-inch version of their motif, and transcribe the clauses from sentences in their latest pieces of writing onto the appropriate parts (see Figure 2–2). Don't be surprised if some of your students who have the most trouble learning the abstractness of clauses are the very ones who are able to come up with the most creative motifs. Just think of the difference this might make to their understanding of clauses.

Materials needed: $8\frac{1}{2}$-by-11-inch paper, markers, scissors, latest pieces of writing

FIG. 2–2 *Artistic clauses*

Help the Poor, Teetering Dependent Clauses

This activity will help your children act out the incomplete feeling a reader gets when reading a dependent clause by itself and the complete feeling she gets from reading an independent clause. To prepare, write sentences from a current text on sentence strips and cut them apart into their clauses. Distribute the clauses to the class. Tell students to stand and read their clause aloud. If they have a dependent clause, they should be feeling like they are teetering back and forth, awaiting something else to anchor the complete thought. If they have an independent clause, they should feel like they are standing firm. Have them act out the feeling they have when they read their clauses. Having thus decided what kind of clause they have been given, the holders of dependent clauses can come to the front and teeter back and forth while calling, "Help! Help!" The holders of independent clauses can look to find the dependent clause that they match and come to the front to "stabilize" the dependent clause and complete the sentence.

Materials needed: sentence strips, markers, scissors, current texts

Decomposition

If your curriculum directs you to teach simple sentences, this activity will be an eye-opener. In a robust program of writing, students often write in compound, complex, and compound-complex sentences without knowing it. Explain what constitutes a simple sentence, then tell students to take the opening sentence of their current draft and rewrite it as a simple sentence. Have them compare their original sentence with the rewritten simple sentence to see which sounds best. Chances are, your students will find the comparison humorous, liking their original sentence better. However, your curricular goal will be met because they will be learning a lesson about simple sentences at the same time.

Materials needed: current pieces of writing, paper and pencils

The Continuing Case of the Tampered Texts

Periodically, add a bit of intrigue to your classroom with another installment of The Continuing Case of the Tampered Texts. Only you will know that you are really sneaking in some more information about and practice in sentence combining, because we won't tell. (Sentence-combining techniques are ways in which authors take short, choppy sentences and combine them into longer, more *meaty* sentences. If you need a quick review, Figure 2–3 lists some of the more common techniques.)

To prepare, choose a short, well-written passage from a text that your students really love—one you currently are using for literature study, real-aloud, or content area study. Rewrite it on a chart or transparency into short, choppy sentences. Emoting for all you are worth, announce that something strange happened overnight. It seems that someone entered the classroom and tampered with a text. Not just any text, but a favorite text. The nerve of this intruder! She took the author's beautiful writing and made a mess of things! Show the rewritten text. Together, discuss ways of combining these sentences to try to recapture the author's beautiful voice. At the end, revisit the author's original version and compare how he wrote it with how the class rewrote it. What sentence-combining techniques did he seem to use? Here is an example from *Harry Potter and the Goblet of Fire* (Rowling 2000, 135), but this activity will work best if you use one of your own texts.

original text: Winky trembled and shook her head frantically, her ears flapping, as Mr. Diggory raised his own wand again and placed it tip to tip with Harry's.

rewritten text: Winky trembled. She shook her head. She was frantic. Her ears flapped. This happened as Mr. Diggory raised his own wand again. He placed it tip to tip with Harry's.

Materials needed: chart paper or transparency, markers, current text, overhead projector

Name that Tune

Because dependent clauses cannot stand alone, they are perfect for this version of Name That Tune. In groups of three or four, students select songs they will use to challenge the class. Because they do not want to give away the song too easily, they identify *dependent* clauses within the lyrics that they will sing for their classmates. Of course, you're really just getting them to pay attention to dependent clauses, but they don't need to know that!

Materials needed: lyrics for student-selected songs

Sentence-Combining Techniques

Use coordinating conjunctions *for, and, nor, but, or,* and *yet* to create compound subjects, verbs, objects, or sentences.

Examples: *Helena takes dancing lessons. Ryley takes dancing lessons.*
(compound subjects) *Helena and Ryley take dancing lessons.*

Tony liked to surf in the afternoons. He liked to fish then, too.
(compound verbs) *Tony liked to surf and fish in the afternoons.*

Ken Sr. likes to tell stories about the good old days. Ken Jr. doesn't like to hear them.
(compound sentence) *Ken Sr. likes to tell stories about the good old days, but Ken Jr. doesn't like to hear them.*

Mrs. Howard makes the best chicken salad. Her coleslaw is really good, too.
(compound objects) *Mrs. Howard makes the best chicken salad and coleslaw.*

Use subordinating conjunctions *although, when, because, since, if,* and so on to create a dependent clause.

Example: *Veronica gets so many phone calls. She always makes time to talk to me.*
(combined) *Although Veronica gets many phone calls, she always makes time to talk to me.*

Use adjectives.

Example: *Harold is a scientist. He is brilliant.*
(combined) *Harold is a brilliant scientist.*

Use appositives.

Example: *Zelda is a Realtor. She has many clients.*
(combined) *Zelda, a Realtor, has many clients.*

Use relative pronouns such as *who, whose, whom,* and *which.*

Example: *That man is a sensational dancer. I can't remember his name.*
(combined) *That man, whose name I can't remember, is a sensational dancer.*

FIG. 2–3   *Sentence-combining techniques*

■ English Language Learners (ELLs), Sentences, and Clauses

As the following chart will show, syntax differs among the languages of the world. We are accustomed to English word order; anything else sounds different or even wrong to our ears. Imagine how *different* or *wrong* English sounds to our ELL learners! Instead of thinking in pejorative terms, let's practice understanding the transference that ELL students must do in order to bridge from their native language to English. It still amazes us when we hear and see the quick progress that ELL students make in our schools. As long as they are prepubescent they soon sound like native English speakers.

In Spanish, Polish, Portuguese, and Greek, word order is much freer than in English. Therefore, your ELL authors may write *Arrived Brad an hour later* instead of *Brad arrived an hour later.*

In Spanish, there is no set word order for questions, and auxiliaries play no part in them. Therefore, your ELL authors may write *Allyson brought the treats?* instead of *Has Allyson brought the treats?*

In Russian, there is no fixed word order in sentences. Therefore, your ELL authors may write sentences in what appears to be totally random word order.

In Portuguese, questions often are formed by adding a questioning word to a declarative sentence or simply by changing intonation. Therefore, your ELL authors may write *Rowena is working now. Yes?* or simply *Rowena is working now,* assuming that the reader will infer a questioning intonation. A nonsubject word often appears at the beginning of a sentence. Therefore, they may write *Girls I like* instead of *I like girls.* Exclamatory sentences use the word order of declarative sentences, with the word *como* (which means *how*) added in the beginning. Therefore, they may write *How Jane is beautiful!* instead of *Jane is so beautiful!*

In Korean and Japanese, the typical word order is subject-object-verb, unlike English, which is ordered subject-verb-object. Therefore, your ELL authors may write *David the ball hit.*

In Korean, Japanese, and Turkish, negative questions are answered with *yes* if the responder agrees with the speaker and *no* if he disagrees. Therefore, your ELL authors may write dialogue such as *Don't you like football? Yes, I really hate it.*

In Japanese, the topic often is placed at the beginning of a declarative sentence. Therefore, your ELL authors may write *Fighting—I do not like at all* instead of *I do not like fighting at all.*

In Farsi, adjectives follow nouns, verbs are at the end of the sentence, and pronouns are omitted if they are understood. Therefore, your ELL authors may write *Yesterday airplane big [I] flew.* In addition, the response to a negative question can be a special retort that translates loosely to *Why not?* This retort often strikes English speakers as flip or abrasive, but it is not meant to be. Therefore, your ELL authors may respond to the question *Don't you want to get an A?* with *Why not?*

In Thai, sentences are written left to right with no spaces between words, and there is no distinction between upper- and lowercase letters. Therefore, your ELL authors may write *sheandhewenthome*.

In Malay-Indonesian, writers often do not write complex sentences. Their language does not lend itself to the use of dependent and independent clauses in the same way English does. Therefore, your ELL authors may have difficulty understanding complex sentences. They may write *Broccoli although bitter but is good for your bones* instead of *Although it is bitter, broccoli is good for your bones*.

(Swan and Smith 2001, 98–9, 118, 122–6, 133, 150, 167–8, 179, 191, 290, 300, 329, 333–4, 348)

Check It Out!

Identify the following sentences as

    A declarative

    B interrogative

    C imperative

    D exclamatory

___1. When did you say that you have class?

___2. Come into the classroom right now.

___3. The classroom is located on the second floor of the red brick building.

___4. This is ridiculous!

Identify the following sentences as

    A simple

    B compound

    C complex

    D compound-complex

___5. Even though she had difficulty reading, she enjoyed the study of literature.

___6. He enjoyed reading high fantasy.

___7. She had difficulty reading, but she enjoyed the study of literature.

___8. Although she had difficulty, she enjoyed the study of literature and she loved to talk about books.

      Answers to test available in Appendix F.

Naming Nouns and Pronouns

What would writing and reading be without the whos, whats, and wheres? That's what nouns and pronouns do for us. They let us know the subjects and objects of what's going on in the sentence. They are common and proper, singular, plural, and collective, and often are indicated by articles like *a, an,* and *the.* A skillful writer knows that strong nouns will anchor the reader in the *who, what,* and *where* of the action he is trying to convey.

You may be thinking, *Yeah, yeah, yeah. A noun is the name of a person, place, or thing. A pronoun replaces a noun. I memorized this in first grade, and second, and third, and tenth. But do I really know it? Do I know how to teach it?* Take heart! Here's a quick review and a host of activities to make nouns and pronouns come alive in your classroom.

Quick Review of Nouns for Teachers

Nouns tell the name of a person (*woman, women*), place (*school, schools*), thing (*desk, desks*), or idea (*love, hate*).

Types of Nouns

Common Nouns: everyday terms; sometimes indicated by an article like *a, an, the.*
    Ex. a woman, an anteater, the school

Proper Nouns: specific names and titles of people, places, and things; are capitalized. *Ex. Dr. Sharon Louis, Los Angeles, California, Honda.*

Collective Nouns: multiple people, places, or things that represent one unit; require a singular verb.
    Ex. team (has), family (goes), group (cheers), crew (races), cache (holds)

Regular Plurals: formed by adding *-s* or *-es. Ex. schools, boxes*

Irregular Plurals: formed by different word forms. *Ex. children, women, oxen*

(Goldstein, Waugh, and Linsky 2004, 205–6; Brandon 2006, 104)

■ Playing with Nouns

Noun Books to Share

Because read-aloud is an integral part of what we believe to be a well-balanced literacy program, we suggest that you share these books with your students. Each is beautifully written. The playfulness with language will trip off your tongue as you explore the world of nouns.

Cleary, Brian P. 1999. *A Mink, a Fink, a Skating Rink: What Is a Noun?* Minneapolis: Carolrhoda.

Heinrichs, Ann. 2004. *Nouns.* Chanhassen, MN: Child's World.

Heller, Ruth. 1987. *A Cache of Jewels and Other Collective Nouns.* New York: Grosset and Dunlap.

———. 1990. *Merry-Go-Round: A Book About Nouns.* New York: Grosset and Dunlap.

Hoban, Tana. 1981. *More than One.* New York: Greenwillow.

MacCarthy, Patricia. 1991. *Herds of Words.* New York: Dial.

Terban, Marvin. 1986. *Your Foot's on My Feet! And Other Tricky Nouns.* New York: Clarion.

Name My Noun

Imagine pretending to be a chair, or the teacher, or the wind. That's exactly what happens in Name My Noun. Students choose nouns from their writing or a current text and act them out while other students have three guesses to name the correct noun. For the previous examples, you just might find children guessing *sitting*, *teaching*, or *whistling*—verbs that describe action. But no! Instead, they must focus on what a noun is—the person, place, or thing that is being represented.

Materials needed: current texts or pieces of writing

Touch Nouns!

Especially useful on those days when it is too wet, snowy, or hot to be outside, Touch Nouns! is a variation on the old game, Statues. Students move around the room until the teacher calls, "Touch nouns!" Students immediately touch a person, place, or thing and freeze. When the teacher says, "Name nouns!" they shout out the name of the noun they are touching.

Materials needed: none

Stand Up for Proper Nouns!

Tell students that proper nouns deserve our respect. When one of them enters the room, we should stand! Read a mixed list of common and proper nouns. When students hear a proper noun, they should stand; when they hear a common noun, they should sit. A bit of activity for times when the wiggles set in!

Materials needed: list of common and proper nouns from current texts

People, Places, and Things

Hand out a sheet of eleven-by-eighteen-inch paper to each student. Ask students to fold their paper into thirds and label each third with either "People," "Places," or "Things." Using old magazines and newspapers, students cut out pictures and place them in the appropriate columns, collage style.

Materials needed: eleven-by-eighteen-inch paper, old magazines and newspapers, glue, scissors, pencils

Super S Saves the Day

Designate one child Super S and give him or her a card with a lowercase *s* printed on it. An old Superman cape (or any piece of capelike material on which you have printed a big S) will help add excitement to this child's role. With a container of popcorn at the ready, have two or more girls at a time come to the front of the room. Place cards with the words *Give   the   girl   some   popcorn* in your pocket chart. Have students discuss what you should do (give popcorn to only one girl). Have the girls call, "Not fair, not fair! We need your help, Super S!" The child portraying Super S sweeps boldly to the front of the room, wielding his or her *s* card and placing it in the pocket chart so that *girl* now says *girls*. Read the sentence again, then give popcorn to the girls standing up front. Repeat with the word cards *Give   the   boy   some   popcorn*. Repeat until all girls and boys have received their share of popcorn. There is quite an impetus for understanding the importance of singular and plural when it means getting popcorn or not!

Materials needed: cards, pocket chart, Superman cape, popcorn, markers

Alphabetica

Alphabetica is an opportunity for your students to uncover how they use nouns in their writing while prompting them to think of possibilities for future pieces of writing as well. Give students a long piece of paper with the letters of the alphabet listed in order down the left side. Have them look through the drafts in their writing folder and list the nouns they have used next to the appropriate beginning letter. Which letter has the most nouns? The least? What kind of pieces might they write that would include nouns beginning with the missing letters? Does that give them any ideas for future pieces?

Materials needed: long pieces of paper with alphabet listed down the side, markers, pencils, students' writing.

Name This Book!

Divide students into small groups. Each group privately identifies a book (or story) that the class has read. The group lists and illustrates significant nouns from that book or story on a piece of poster board labeled "Name This Book!" Number each poster and hang it in the hallway outside the classroom. Give each group an opportunity to go to the hallway to view the posters and complete a Name This Book! answer sheet. After the class has completed the activity, have each group fold a piece of construction paper in half and write the title of the book and the author on the inside. Attach these beneath the posters so that other students in the school can play Name This Book! and check their answers.

Materials needed: authentic texts, poster board, construction paper, crayons or markers

Crazy Compound Nouns

Using three-by-five-inch cards, write half of a compound word on each. Shuffle them and have students each draw a card. Without showing their cards, they line up in two lines facing each other. At a signal from you, they walk straight across and meet a partner. The partners then put their two compound halves together to form a crazy compound. Each pair then goes to the board, writes their crazy compound word, and sketches a picture of what it would be. (See Figure 3–1.) Not enough board space? Just use paper instead. Halves of real compound words such as *moonlight*, *sunshine*, *cowboy*, *doorbell*, *cupcake*, *spaceship*, and *rainfall* recombine in interesting ways. A *cowlight*, for example, might be a battery-powered light that cows wear around their necks so the farmer can see them at night. *Doorshine* might be a special wax meant especially

FIG. 3–1   *Crazy compound nouns*

for making doors look welcoming to visitors. And astronauts certainly could use *space-cups* that attached to their spacesuits so their drinks wouldn't float away. While this activity may seem silly, something bigger is at hand. It requires thinking outside the box, a skill that will be sorely needed as today's children grow up in an increasingly complex world. And who knows? The seed of an invention might even plant itself in one of your young minds.

Materials needed: three-by-five-inch cards, markers, chalkboard and chalk

Numbered Nouns

Numbered Nouns is a variation of the childhood favorite Mad Libs. Students number the nouns in their latest piece of writing, then copy them onto a separate piece of paper (e.g., "I gave my dog a bath last night and got water all over the floor" would yield the list 1. dog, 2. bath, 3. night, 4. water, 5. floor). Next, they exchange lists with a partner and read their piece aloud, substituting their partner's numbered nouns for their own. Hilarity ensues when a sentence like "Seven *people* came to my *party* last *Saturday* and we ate a lot of *pizza* and *cupcakes*" becomes "Seven *dog*[s] came to my *bath* last *night* and we ate a lot of *water* and *floor*[s]"!

Materials needed: students' writing, paper and pencils

Making the Common Uncommonly Good

Have students identify a common noun in a piece of their writing and write it, and the sentence in which it occurred, at the top of a piece of paper. On a signal from you, they pass their paper to the student next to them. The next child reads the sentence and writes a more specific noun that might replace the common noun on the paper. Signal again to pass the paper to the next child, who will do the same. Continue as long as interest is high and productive nouns are being generated. Students may use thesauri, dictionaries, classroom word charts, or any other source if needed. The common word *car*, for example, might generate a list that would include *Ford*, *Saturn*, *vehicle*, *wheels*, and so forth. The writer, of course, has the ultimate say in what noun she will use, but she'll have several options from which to choose.

Materials needed: students' writing, paper and pencils, thesauri, dictionaries, classroom word charts

Nine Notable Nouns

Use a current piece of fiction or nonfiction text that students are reading or writing and have students each choose the nine notable nouns that are central to this piece, share them with a partner, and justify why they chose them. This activity not only underscores nouns but also requires students to think carefully about the meaning of the text they are reading. The result? Noun knowledge and critical comprehension.

Materials needed: current texts, paper and pencils

Opposites Attract

Nouns that represent qualities or ideas are the most difficult to recognize because they are abstract. Thinking about them in pairs helps. Prepare cards with abstract nouns on them, making sure that you have a card for each noun's opposite as well. For example, you might use words like *war/peace, love/hate, truth/lies, slavery/freedom, hope/despair, happiness/sadness, cleanliness/dirtiness, beauty/ugliness,* and *height/depth, tragedy/comedy, length/width, obesity/gauntness, formality/casualness, admission/denial, praise/criticism, illness/health.* Distribute one card to each student. Holding their card in front of them, students silently walk around the room looking for their opposite. When opposites think they have found each other, they confirm their choice by looking in a dictionary or a dictionary of antonyms.

Materials needed: cards, marker, dictionaries

Abstract Acting

If you already have made the cards for the Opposites Attract activity described above, you have another activity ready to go with no further effort on your part. Divide students into pairs and give each a pair of opposite abstract nouns. Whispering together so that the rest of the class can't hear, they plan how they will act out their pair of words. When it's showtime, each pair performs and the rest of the class guesses their abstract noun pair.

Materials needed: cards from Opposites Attract

Names for Things and How They Got That Way

Cupboard, closet, armoire, cabinet, chiffonier, chifforobe, and *wardrobe* all are names for places where we store things. Challenge your students to find the languages of origin for these synonyms and others. Invite them to interview people to find out what they call such commonplace items as sofas, eyeglasses, faucets, toilets, baby carriages, and so forth. Then they can report their findings to the class. This activity also encourages your ELL students to add their language to the whole class' understanding of nouns.

Materials needed: paper and pencils, dictionaries

A Collection of Collectives

Collective nouns like *class, team,* and *family* are quite familiar, but they are just a few of the many interesting and unusual terms in use. Collective terms originated with hunters, who needed to have a way to describe their quarries of field and game animals. This helps explain why animals have specific nouns that name their groups— a *down* of hares, a *bevy* of quail, a *brace* of grouse, for example. Appendix C contains a list of collective terms. Challenge your students to use dictionaries and other references to figure out what the collective nouns refer to. Choose the most common, or give them the entire list to work on over a period of weeks.

Materials needed: list of collective nouns, reference materials

Walking in Authors' Footsteps: Proper Nouns

Authors use proper nouns for more than naming people and places. For example, Ray (1999) notes how proper nouns give Cynthia Rylant's *Missing May* (1992) so much more sensory power in this passage: "My eyes went over May's wildly colorful cabinets, and I was free again. I saw Oreos and Ruffles and big bags of Snickers" (4). Yes, she could have written the common nouns *cookies, chips,* and *candy bars*, but not with the same impact. Share this sentence from *Missing May* and ask students to name the common nouns that *Oreos, Ruffles,* and *Snickers* represent. Compare two versions of that sentence—one using common nouns, the other using proper nouns. Share one of your drafts in which you replace common nouns with proper nouns in order to heighten the reader's vision of what you have written. Have students choose a draft from their writing folder and find a sentence that could be made stronger by substituting proper for common nouns. Share and discuss these sentences. In your discussion, you may find that proper nouns do not *always* improve a sentence, and that's fine. The value of this activity is the discussion that takes place—one that presents a craft strategy that *might* be useful in future writing while simultaneously reinforcing the grammar you are studying.

Materials needed: authentic texts, teacher's writing, students' writing

Mommy Hugs

Have your upper-grade students prepare to read and share *Mommy Hugs* (Gutman and Hallensleben 2003) with younger children. Your colleagues who teach the younger ones might just welcome a visit from your students, and if your students are starting to baby-sit, their young charges will love hearing this sweet tale. *Mommy Hugs* is a story of mother-child love, with a simplistic text that will take your students back to an earlier time in their lives. It tells of mommies (cat, parrot, polar bear, elephant, swan, monkey) who hug their babies (kitten, chick, cub, calf, cygnet, baby) in special ways (with a nuzzle, with a nibble, with a tickle, with a squeeze, with a cuddle, with a pat). Revisit this story with your class and have the students help you make a chart with three columns of nouns, labeled "Mommies," "Babies," and "With a _____." The nouns in the first column function as subjects. In the second column, the nouns are objects. In the third, they are objects in prepositional phrases. The text is simplistic, but the concepts about nouns are not. Ostensibly, your students will be preparing to share a book, but they will be reviewing rather sophisticated noun understandings at the same time.

Materials needed: several copies of *Mommy Hugs*, chart paper, marker

Quick Review of Pronouns for Teachers

Pronouns take the place of nouns to keep the author from using the same noun over and over. *Ex. Allyson works very hard. She is known for her dedication. Her work is an example for all.*

Pronoun Case

Subjective or Nominative: pronouns used as the subject.
> *Ex. She went to the store. They couldn't wait.*

Objective: pronouns used as the object. *Ex. Give the guitar to him.*

Possessive: pronouns that indicate possession.
> *Ex. His name is on the envelope. The house is theirs.*

Singular and Plural Pronouns

Singular pronouns replace singular nouns. Plural pronouns replace plural nouns. Here's how they work:

First Person Subjective: *I* (singular), *we* (plural)

First Person Objective: *me* (singular), *us* (plural)

First Person Possessive: *my, mine* (singular), *our, ours* (plural)

Second Person Subjective: *you* (the same for both singular and plural)

Second Person Objective: *you* (the same for both singular and plural)

Second Person Possessive: *your, yours* (the same for both singular and plural)

Third Person Subjective: *he, she, it* (singular), *they* (plural)

Third Person Objective: *him, her, it* (singular), *them* (plural)

Third Person Possessive: *his, her, hers, its* (singular), *their, theirs* (plural)

Types of Pronouns

Personal:	*I, my, mine, me* (singular), *we, our, ours, us* (plural)
	you, your, yours (singular and plural)
	he, his, him, she, her, hers, it, its (singular), *they, their, theirs, them* (plural)
Interrogative:	*who, whose, whom, which, what*
Relative:	*who, whose, whom, which, what, that, whoever, whomever, whichever, whatever*
Demonstrative:	*this, that, these, those*
Indefinite:	*another, anybody, anyone, anything, each, either, everybody, everyone, everything, neither, nobody, no one, nothing, one, somebody, someone, something* (singular)

both, few, many, others, several (plural)

all, any, more, most, none, some, such (singular or plural)

Reciprocal: *each other, one another* (plural)

Reflexive and Intensive: *myself, yourself, himself, herself, itself,* (singular)
ourselves, themselves, yourselves (plural)

Pronouns as Appositives

Intensive pronouns often are used as *appositives* for emphasis. *Ex. I, myself, am responsible for the mishap.*

(Ellsworth and Higgins 2004, 13)

■ Playing with Pronouns

Pronoun Books to Share

You will hear *your* students yell, "*We* love *these* books. *They* are great!" when *you* read *them.*

> Cleary, Brian P. 2004. *I and You and Don't Forget Who: What Is a Pronoun?*
> Illustrated by Brian Gable. Minneapolis: Carolrhoda.

> Heinrichs, Ann. 2004. *Pronouns.* Chanhassen, MN: Child's World.

> Heller, Ruth. 1997. *Mine All Mine: A Book About Pronouns.* New York: Grosset
> and Dunlap.

Politeness Only, Please

"Put others first," said our mothers, and so it is with pronouns. It's *Howie and I would like a drink,* not *Me and Howie* or *I and Howie.* It's *Give the cookies to Linda and me,* not *to me and Linda* or *to I and Linda.* Think of the times during the day when your students need to request things of you. Stopping for a drink? Have pairs say, "Kathy and I would like a drink," in order to get your permission to step up to the fountain. Passing out papers? Have pairs say, "Please give the papers to Bill and me." Use every minute of your day to practice politeness and pronouns.

Materials needed: none

Hey, Pronouns, Stand Up!

Pronouns stand in for nouns. In this activity, that's exactly what your students will do. Tell them that they are all pronouns. Have them listen while you read a passage from a current text out loud. Whenever they hear a pronoun, they should stand.

Materials needed: current text

In, Out, and In Again

Whether you're in or out in this game is just the luck of the draw, but it really reinforces nominative and objective pronoun cases. Play is very simple. Students stand in a circle and pass a container filled with sentence cards on which you have written correctly and incorrectly used pronouns. When the container comes to a student, he draws a card and reads it aloud. If his card is correct, he remains standing; if his card is incorrect, he sits. After reading a card, the student returns it to the container. Keep playing until there is only one student standing. Then reverse the game, so that when someone draws a correct card, she can stand up. Play until everyone is standing up again. Following are sentence suggestions for this game.

Doug and I like to read books.

Fred and I had lunch.

He and I thought it was sad.

She and I like to shop.

Give the job to Gloria and me.

I picked out a gift for him and her.

Everyone likes him and me.

Those pears are not ripe.

They went home.

Pass the papers to her and me.

When it's raining, I like to stay inside.

Mike played soccer with them and me.

We the people of the United States . . .

Give them a chance.

Me and Sammy are going swimming.

Jeff and me played catch.

Run quickly with Fido and she.

Trade places with her and I.

Patty and them threw a party for us.

Us kids don't like tests.

Them people aren't coming.

Them and her started to laugh.

Six candy bars aren't enough for they and I.

Meet he and I at six o'clock.

Materials needed: sentence cards, marker, container

Interactive Pronoun Practice

This is the type of practice exercise that many of us remember, but with an interactive, self-checking twist. Write the following sentences on sentence strips and place them in a pocket chart. Next to each one, place cards with the possible choices for filling in the blank. Place a ☺ on the back of the correct choice and an X on the back of the incorrect choices. Students read each sentence and select the card they believe to be correct, then self-check by turning it over.

1. Dori touched the turtle on _____ shell. (it's, **its**, its')

2. The first prize went to Roberto and _____ . (I, **me**)

3. Dr. Josephs gave us—_____—the best grade. (**Amanda and me**, Amanda and I)

4. Only _____ Philadelphians know about the ups and downs of football. (us, **we**)

5. _____ bookbags are clear plastic. (They're, **Their**, There)

6. Pat was bothered by _____ coughing. (**his**, him)

7. To _____ does this test belong? (who, **whom**)

8. Invite _____ you want to Barbara's party. (whoever, **whomever**)

9. _____ is my desk. (**This/That**, These/Those)

10. Dennis did the project by _____. (hisself, **himself**)

11. It is _____. (**I**, me)

Materials needed: sentence strips, pocket chart, cards, marker

Silent Pronoun Auction

You can get double duty from the Interactive Pronoun Practice activity by having a Silent Pronoun Auction after everyone has had a turn at the pocket chart. In silent auctions, which often occur at fund-raising events, you purchase tickets and place them in boxes located in front of various prizes. At the end of the evening the master of ceremonies draws a ticket from each box to see who has won the silent auction for that prize. Instead of a box, place an envelope at the beginning of each sentence. Instead of tickets, give each student a small slip of paper for each sentence. Independently, students write the correct word for each sentence (along with their name) on a slip of paper and then deposit the slips in the appropriate envelopes. After all students have entered their words, you check each envelope and leave the correct responses inside. With fanfare, then, you reach into each envelope and pull a slip of paper to see which student will win a small prize (one per sentence). This activity also allows you to see who has not contributed the appropriate words and needs further instruction.

Materials needed: Interactive Pronoun Practice sentence strips, pocket chart, envelopes, slips of paper, pencils

Whom Do You Mean?

Authors get into trouble when they don't use the proper pronoun reference. This confuses readers because they don't know who or what is being talked about. Consider this sentence: *Dan gave the baby his drink.* What did the baby drink?— Dan's scotch and soda, or the baby's formula? To whom does the pronoun *his* refer? Have students take a draft from their writing folders and underline the pronouns, then exchange papers with a partner. Over each pronoun, in pencil, each student writes the noun she thinks her partner meant. When the owners receive their papers back, they check to see if they have been understood the way they intended. In the example sentence, the partner might pencil in *Dan* over the pronoun *his*, causing the author to say, "No, I meant the baby!" Such *ahas* provide authentic motivation to revise the construction of an entire sentence to make the meaning clear. Without a reader, though, the poor author might never know.

Materials needed: students' writing, pencils

What If There Were No Pronouns?

Pronouns serve the writer and protect the ears of the reader from an assault of repeated nouns. Look at two versions of the same passage:

Version 1

Sandy asked Donna if she would like to go shopping with her. Donna said she would love to, but first she would have to go to her bank. Sandy chuckled and said to herself, "She had better withdraw a lot of money because I know how she likes to shop."

Version 2

Sandy asked Donna if Donna would like to go shopping with Sandy. Donna said Donna would love to, but first Donna would have to go to Donna's bank. Sandy chuckled and said to Sandy, "Donna had better withdraw a lot of money because Sandy knows how Donna likes to shop."

Version 1 was much simpler, and more natural, to write and to read. For that, we thank pronouns. Tell students that today they will see what a world without pronouns would be like. Use a short passage from a current text and model two versions of it, one with pronouns and one without. Give students another sentence from the text that contains pronouns and have them rewrite it without pronouns. Then have them choose a sentence or two from their writing to play with in the same fashion. Along the way, they just might clarify their pronoun reference as well.

Materials needed: current text, students' writing, paper and pencils

Walking in Authors' Footsteps: Pronouns

Vague pronoun reference can be a problem. However, sometimes authors use this vagueness on purpose. Ray (1999) notes, for example, that Cynthia Rylant consistently avoids using a possessive pronoun in front of the word *relatives* in *The Relatives*

Came (1985a). They are not *our* relatives or *her* or *his* relatives, but *the* relatives, adding to the *this-could-be-anyone's-story* universal appeal of her book. Likewise, Rylant is intentionally vague when she writes, "They are floating like feathers in *a* sky" (n.p.) in *The Whales* (1985b). Why? Is she suggesting that there could be more than one sky? Is she purposefully comparing the sea and the sky? Questions such as these certainly will lead to rich discussions with your class, and a deeper understanding of pronouns as well. Present these sentences, and others from your current texts, to your students. Ask them to speculate why the authors chose to use intentional vagueness. In what situations might this work and not work? Share sentences from your own writing, and invite your students to do the same. Compare what would happen if they used a vague pronoun versus a specific term. What effect would it have on the reader?

Materials needed: authentic texts, teacher's writing, students' writing

It's at the End

What's at the end? Anything you want. You see, *it* is whatever is at the end of the path on this board game. Have pairs of students each make a board game on an open file folder. Together, they decide the theme. The object of the game will be to get to the end of the path, where perhaps a pot of gold awaits, or a candy house, or a jet. They illustrate their board game according to the theme, drawing whatever *it* is at the end of the path. Make small cards on which you have written sentences or phrases that contain correct and incorrect usage of the singular pronoun *it*, the possessive pronoun *its*, and the often misused contraction *it's*. When each pair has a set of cards, go over the phrases with the class to indicate which are correctly written and which are not. Students write *yes* on the back of each correctly written card and *no* on the back of the incorrectly written cards. Each pair places the playing cards sentence side–up. Rolling a die or spinning a spinner, players take turns moving forward along the path. Before they can move, however, they must pick up a card and tell whether the sentence is correct as written or not, confirming by looking on the back of the card. If they confirm that they were right, they move ahead; if not, they stay where they are. The first one to reach *it* at the end of the path wins that round of the game. Store the cards in resealable food storage bags so that the games can be played again, traded with other pairs, or taken home to play with the family.

Materials needed: file-folder game boards, cards, markers, spinners (or dice), playing pieces, resealable food storage bags

I Me My Mine

Susan Van Zile contributed this great idea to *Instructor* in an article called "Grammar That'll Move You" (2003). To the tune of "YMCA," substitute pronouns with motions that point to the referent. What ones shall you group together? Edgar Schuster (2003, 23–26) suggests displaying a personal pronoun chart in the classroom, a chart that he hypothesizes is close to the one that "hangs somewhere in the human brain" (26). We have included it in Figure 3–2. At a glance, it lists the

A Personal Pronoun Chart

____ saw the cats.	The cats saw ____.	____ snack was good.	The snack is ____.	(self/selves)
Singular				
I	*me*	*my*	*mine*	*myself*
you	*you*	*your*	*yours*	*yourself*
she	*her*	*her*	*hers*	*herself*
he	*him*	*his*	*his*	*himself*
it	*it*	*its*	*its*	*itself*
Plural				
we	*us*	*our*	*ours*	*ourselves*
you	*you*	*your*	*yours*	*yourselves*
they	*them*	*their*	*theirs*	*themselves*

FIG. 3–2 *Edgar Schuster's Personal Pronoun Chart*

singular and plural personal pronouns in a concise reference, useful in test-crazed schools. Singing across the rows or down the columns would constructively fill the two minutes here and the three minutes there while you wait for the clock to signal time for lunch, time to go to art class, and so forth.

Materials needed: pronoun chart

Jack and His House of Relative Pronouns

Raise your students' understanding of relative pronouns by sharing the book *This Is the House That Jack Built* (Taback 2002). The text evolves as a cumulative tale with a repetitive structure that goes like this: "This is the rat that ate the cheese that lay in the house that Jack built" (n.p.). Modeled after a sixteenth-century Hebrew chant, *This Is the House That Jack Built* was first published in 1755 and was later illustrated by none other than Randolph Caldecott in 1878. After you read this story just for the fun of hearing it again, your students can revisit its use of the relative pronouns such as *that* and *who*. Explain what a relative pronoun is, then examine how *that* and *who* were used in this particular text. Have students create their own cumulative tales involving themselves, titled *The _____ That [Name] _____.* ("This is the cat that Richard adopted." "This is Barbara, whose mother, Marie, married her father, John, who built the treehouse.")

Materials needed: authentic text, paper and pencils, pronoun list

Patriotic Pronouns

The social studies curriculum in the upper-elementary and middle school grades often focuses on American history and government. This is a perfect time to sing some patriotic songs, past and present, and practice pronouns as well. If you examine the lyrics of "My Country 'Tis of Thee," "This Land Is Your Land," "When Johnny Comes Marching Home," and many others, you will find a treasure of pronouns—*I, my, me, thee, him, our* and more. Look at the lyrics and identify the types of pronouns. Talk about old forms of pronouns, such as *thee* and *thou*.

Materials needed: song lyrics

■ English Language Learners, Nouns, and Pronouns

English is a polyglot language, having borrowed words from the native languages of all who came to and interacted with the English-speaking world. Names for persons, places, and things in English really reflect multiple languages and give us interchangeable names for the same thing. For example, *sofa, divan, davenport, loveseat, futon, settee,* and *couch* all indicate that article of furniture found in most living rooms. These multiple names for items can pose difficulty for ELL students whose native languages do not display such variety. In addition, many languages use pronouns much differently than English does, particularly in matters of gender and number.

In Spanish, nouns have gender that is indicated by an article, either *la* (feminine) or *el* (masculine). Therefore, your ELL authors may add articles in their writing that are not needed (*going to the skiing* rather than *going skiing*). The word for *people* is *la gente*, and it is singular. Therefore, your ELL authors may use a singular verb with people (*The people is having fun*). Subject personal pronouns are not used because the verb ending indicates the person and number. Therefore, your ELL authors may write *Sandy is not Hungarian. Is American.* instead of *Sandy is not Hungarian. She is American.* There is no equivalent for the contraction *It's* + pronoun. Therefore, your ELL authors may write *Am I* instead of *It's I* (or *me*). *That, which,* and *who* all are equivalent to the Spanish *que*. Therefore, your ELL authors may write *The boy which threw the ball.*

In Vietnamese, there is no article before the name of a profession. Therefore, your ELL authors may write *He is professor*.

In Japanese, pronouns do not have to match their nouns in terms of singular and plural. Therefore, your ELL authors may need instruction in how to use plurals such as *we, they,* and *them.*

In Japanese and Cantonese, there are no articles or inflections for person and number. Therefore, your ELL authors may write *Student miss two class.*

In Swahili, speakers do not distinguish between masculine and feminine pronoun forms. Therefore, your ELL authors may confuse *he* and *she, him* and *her* when they write. In addition, a pronoun often is used after a noun, seeming redundant. Therefore, your ELL authors may write *The girls they kick the ball* instead of *The girls kick the ball.*

In Korean, pronouns do not have gender. Therefore, your ELL authors may write the neutral pronoun *it* to refer to both males and females.

In Chinese, speakers drop pronouns that are understood. Therefore, your ELL authors may write *I sang the song before took the bow* instead of *I sang the song before I took the bow.*

In Portuguese, speakers frequently drop subjective pronouns. Therefore, your ELL authors may write *Don't want to go* instead of *I don't want to go.* Objective pronouns may be omitted if they are understood through context. Therefore, your ELL authors may write *Marlene and Warren can dance. I've seen.* instead of *Marlene and Warren can dance. I've seen them.* In addition, the impersonal pronoun *it* does not exist. Therefore, your ELL authors may write *When Bonnie laughs, is hard to stop her* instead of *When Bonnie laughs, it is hard to stop her.*

In Farsi, a single pronoun is used for both *he* and *she*. Therefore, your ELL authors may write *Audrey is an artist. He works in oils.*

(Swan and Smith 2001, 105, 124, 189, 272, 319; Haussaman 2003, 52–5)

Check It Out!

Identify the type of noun represented by the underlined words in this student-written letter.

Dear **<u>Zelig</u>**,

I heard that you were thinking of going back to **<u>school</u>** to study **<u>Chinese</u>**. Will you be studying **<u>Mandarin</u>** or **<u>Cantonese</u>**? Many **<u>people</u>** enjoy the study of languages. I know that it will come easily to you because you know several **<u>languages</u>** already. Let me wish you the best of luck. Please keep me posted and let me know about your progress.

Sincerely,

Pam

Identify the underlined pronouns in this student-written journal entry:

Journal Entry for November 11

1. Today **<u>I</u>** attended **<u>my</u>** first Veterans' Day celebration. 2. **<u>I</u>** was moved to hear the Veterans of several wars talk about **<u>their</u>** experiences. 3. **<u>It</u>** was not just a ceremony where **<u>they</u>** laid wreaths on tombs.

4. **<u>These</u>** men talked and talked about **<u>their</u>** feelings. The Vietnam Vets were especially interesting.

5. While **<u>I</u>** was not alive to witness the happenings, **<u>it</u>** is clear that **<u>these</u>** men were not treated fairly.

6. **<u>I</u>** wanted to hug **<u>them</u>** and tell **<u>them</u>**, "Thank you," but **<u>I</u>** was too embarrassed to do that.

7. **<u>Who</u>** would deserve an award more than **<u>these</u>** veterans? 8. **<u>Everyone</u>** that was there would agree with **<u>me</u>**. 9. For **<u>myself</u>**, let **<u>me</u>** just say that **<u>I</u>** really felt appreciation after **<u>I</u>** heard the men speak.

Answers to test available in Appendix F.

Vivid Verbs

As important as nouns and pronouns are, it is the verb in the sentence that propels the meaning. Weak verbs leave the reader confused or uninterested, but strong verbs draw the reader in to what is happening in a piece of writing. Authors know that verbs represent the very heart of their writing, and they put at least one of them in almost every sentence. Even in a one-word sentence like *Stop!* that word is a verb because the subject, *you*, is understood.

At their essence, verbs show action (*eats, ate*) or state of being (*is, was*). But there is much more to know! Verbs are very busy words. They take on tenses, affect direct and indirect objects, help out other verbs, and sometimes even function as nouns. You may be thinking, *This sounds pretty complicated. Am I up to teaching this?* Relax. We'll give you a brief review and lots of activities for getting your students to know and love this exciting little part of speech.

Quick Review for Teachers

Two Basic Functions of Verbs

Action Verbs: show action.
> **Transitive Verbs:** show action being done to something or someone else. The someone or something can be a direct object. *Ex. Dori* (subject) *returned* (transitive verb) *the book* (direct object). It also may be an indirect object.
>> *Ex. I* (subject) *told* (transitive verb) *Katie* (indirect object) *a secret* (direct object).
>
> **Intransitive Verbs:** stand alone; show action without the need for a direct or indirect object. *Ex. Dori* (subject) *returned* (intransitive verb).

Being Verbs: show state of being.
> **Helping Verbs** (also called auxiliary verbs): help show tense. *Ex.*
>
> | | | |
> |---|---|---|
> | *have* | *shall* | *might* |
> | *be (am, is)* | *should* | *must* |
> | *do* | *can* | *have (to)* |
> | *will* | *could* | *ought (to)* |
> | *would* | *may* | *need (to)* |

Linking Verbs (also called state-of-being verbs): show relationship between a subject and an object. *Ex. Alisa is a doctor. Penelope was the manager.*

Tenses

The Simple Tenses
Present: use the main verb for all pronouns except for *he*, *she*, or *it*. For *he*, *she*, or *it*, add *-s* or *-es*. *Ex.*

Singular	**Plural**
I learn.	*We learn.*
You learn.	*You learn.*
He, she, it learns.	*They learn.*

Past: use the main verb and add *-ed* for all forms.
Ex. I/You/He/She/It/We/You/They learned.

Future: use *shall* or *will* plus the main verb. *Ex. I/He/You They shall/will learn.*

The Perfect Tenses (*Has, Have, or Had*)
Present Perfect: use *have* or *has* plus the main verb with the *-ed* ending.
Ex. I/We/You/They have learned. He/She/It has learned.

Past Perfect: use *had* plus the main verb with the *-ed* ending.
Ex. I/We/You/They/He/She/It had learned.

Future Perfect: use *shall/will have* plus the main verb with the *-ed* ending.
Ex. I/We/You/They/He/She/It will have learned.

The Progressive Tenses
Present Progressive: indicates action *in progress now*.
Ex. I am learning. He/She/It is learning. They/You/We are learning.

Past Progressive: indicates action that was *in progress in the past*.
Ex. I/He/She/It was learning. They/You/We were learning.

Future Progressive: indicates action that will be *in progress in the future*.
Ex. I/You/He/She/They/We/It will be learning.

The Perfect Progressive Tenses
Present Perfect Progressive: indicates *progress up to now*.
Ex. I/You/They/We have been learning. He/She/It has been learning.

Past Perfect Progressive: indicates action that was *in progress before something else in the past*. *Ex. I/You/He/She/It/They/We had been learning.*

Future Perfect Progressive: indicates action that *will be in progress before something else in the future*. *Ex. I/You/He/She/It/They/We will have been learning.*

Regular Versus Irregular Verbs

Regular Verbs: form past tense and past participles (using helping verbs such as *can, do, does, did, may, might, must, shall, should, will,* and *would*) by adding *-ed* to the main verb.

Irregular Verbs: change words for past tense and participles.

Main Verb	Past	Past Participle
go	*went*	*gone*
freeze	*froze*	*frozen*
buy	*bought*	*bought*
know	*knew*	*known*
say	*said*	*said*
take	*took*	*taken*
write	*wrote*	*written*
run	*ran*	*run*
throw	*threw*	*thrown*
see	*saw*	*seen*
shake	*shook*	*shaken*
wear	*wore*	*worn*
steal	*stole*	*stolen*
ride	*rode*	*ridden*
come	*came*	*come*
do	*did*	*done*
forget	*forgot*	*forgotten*

Verbals

Verbals are verbs that function as nouns (subjects and objects).
>   **Gerunds:** Verb + *-ing* acting as a noun (subject or object).
>   > *Ex. Swimming is good exercise. I like swimming.*
>   **Infinitives:** *To* + the main form of a verb acting as a noun (subject or object).
>   > *Ex. To err is human. I like to swim.*

(Ellsworth and Higgins 2004, 5–9; Brandon 2006, 89–90)

■ Playing with Verbs

Verb Books to Share

Read! Savor! Enjoy! Have a good time sharing these books with your children. Verbs come to life in the pages of these books.

Beller, Janet. 1984. *A-B-Cing: An Action Alphabet.* New York: Crown.

Burningham, John. 1986. *Cluck Baa, Jangle Twang, Slam Bang, Skip Trip, Sniff Shout, Wobble Pop.* New York: Viking.

Heinrichs, Ann. 2004. *Verbs*. Chanhassen, MN: Child's World.

Heller, Ruth. 1988. *Kites Sail High: A Book About Verbs*. New York: Grosset and Dunlap.

Maestro, Betsy. 1985. *Camping Out*. Illustrated by Giulio Maestro. New York: Crown.

Neumeier, Marty, and Byron Glasser. 1985. *Action Alphabet*. New York: Greenwillow.

Rotner, Shelley. 1996. *Action Alphabet*. New York: Atheneum.

Schneider, R. M. 1995. *Add It, Dip It, Fix It: A Book of Verbs*. Boston: Houghton Mifflin.

Shierman, Vicky. 1981. *M Is for Move*. New York: Dutton.

Terban, Marvin. 1984. *I Think I Thought and Other Tricky Verbs*. New York: Clarion.

The Big Bad -ing

This is a spelling story to help your students remember to double the final consonant when creating the past-tense and participle forms of verbs that have a short vowel sound. If your students balk at the silliness of this story, consider having them prepare this as a creative activity to share with primary-grade buddies. Choose any verb whose final consonant must be doubled before adding *-ed* and *-ing*, for example, *bat*. Make a letter card for each of the letters—a large *b* and *t*, but a very small *a*. (The *a* is short, remember?) In addition, make an extra *t* for the doubling process and an *ed* card and an *ing* card for the inflected endings. (By turning the *ed* and the *ing* into faces with jagged teeth and snarls, you can make this story even more dramatic.) Pass out the cards. First, call the *b* card to come forward. Then, invite the *little, tiny, short a* to come forward to the sound effects of "Awww . . . isn't he cute . . . just a short little thing . . ." to cement the notion of *short*. (Yes, it's a different kind of short, but we're trying to make something abstract more concrete.) Then call for one *t* to complete the word. Tell the class that a big, bad *-ing* roams the land with his equally diabolical partner *-ed*. They love to terrorize little, defenseless short vowels and then eat them up! When this happens, the final consonant has to call for her twin sister. Together, they stand arm in arm to keep the predators away from the short vowel.

Then, the action begins. Have the bloodthirsty *ed* and *ing* cards lumber forward in large ogrelike steps, howling and growling. As this is happening, have the little short *a* begin to tremble. As the fiends grow near, have the final consonant call "Twin *t*! Twin *t*! Come quickly! We must protect the little short vowel!" And, of course, the second *t* arrives just in time, joining arms with his twin to provide the needed safety barrier and to save the day. (See Figure 4–1.)

Materials needed: cards, marker

FIG. 4–1   *The Big Bad* -ing

Is It OK to Use Said or Isn't It?

Students often overuse the word *said* when writing dialogue. Use three simple texts, *Hattie and the Fox* (Fox 1986), *The Little Red Hen* (Barton 1993), and *The Very Busy Spider* (Carle 1984), to compare and contrast how authors use the word *said* and its alternatives to create compelling tales. Mem Fox uses *said* over and over in *Hattie and the Fox* ("Good grief!" said the goose; "Well, well," said the pig; "Who cares?" said the sheep; and so on). Barton avoids the word *said* altogether, choosing instead to use more specific verbs ("Not I," squealed the pig; "Not I," quacked the duck; "Not I," meowed the cat). Carle intersperses *said* with words such as *bleated* and *grunted*. Ask students to evaluate these authors' verb choices and to think about why they might have made them. Do these texts work? What makes them work? How would they sound if their authors had made other choices? Have students revise Mem Fox's work, substituting different verbs for *said*, in the manner of Barton or Carle. (For example, "Good grief," honked the goose; "Well, well," oinked the pig.) Which sounds better? Why? Have students reflect on their own writing. What other words might they use instead of *said*? Why? List these possibilities on a chart.

Materials needed: authentic texts, class list of verbs, students' writing, paper and pencils

Napping Ways

In *The Napping House* (1984), Audrey Wood describes a house in which everyone naps in a special way. The tale unfolds in cumulative fashion, and just before the story's climax, the reader discovers that *"[on a] mouse there is a flea. Can it be? A wakeful flea on a slumbering mouse on a snoozing cat on a dozing dog on a dreaming child on a snoring granny on a cozy bed in a napping house, where everyone is sleeping"* (n.p.). As you might have guessed, the flea bites the mouse, and that triggers a chain reaction until *no one is napping* anymore. For younger students, the text is just right for a written retelling featuring verbs. After reading it just for enjoyment, have students dictate or write about the characters while you read it for a second time. For example, *The granny is snoring; The child is dreaming; The dog is dozing*; and so forth. Call attention to the different words that Wood uses for *napping*. While this clearly is a story for younger children, you can use it to reinforce more sophisticated grammar. The verb participles that are synonyms for *napping* are used as adjectives in this story—a source for a good minilesson in itself. Make a list of them—a *slumbering* mouse, a *dreaming* child—and talk about this unique use of verb participles.

Materials needed: authentic text, chart paper, marker

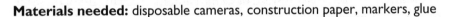

Photo Montage

Send home disposable cameras and have students photograph actions that are part of their environments. Students can mount the developed pictures on construction paper and label them with the verbs that occur in their daily lives.

Materials needed: disposable cameras, construction paper, markers, glue

Bookmarks

Bring verbs to life by looking at how published authors use them. Give each student a bookmark made from oak tag for the novel or content area text the students currently are reading. Divide the bookmarks into categories, based upon what you are studying about verbs (for example, "Active," "Passive," "Helping," "Irregular"). As they read an assigned section, students list the verbs their author uses under the appropriate heading. Thanks to the "Green Pages" (Swartz 2003) in the January 2003 issue of *Teaching K–8* for this great idea!

Materials needed: oak tag bookmarks, current texts, pencils

The Helpful Helping Verbs

Save that gold or silver tinsel garland from Christmas trees past, because it will make a great halo when tied in a circle and placed on top of a child's head. And halos are just what you will need for celebrating the goodness of helping verbs. Appoint two children to be the helping verbs *is* and *are*. Each of them gets to wear a halo with a card attached bearing the word *is* or *are*. (Writing the words in glitter pen or something equally celestial will just add to the goodness. If you have access to old white acolyte cottas that they can wear, it only gets better.) You'll need cards on which you have written the pronouns *He*, *She*, and *They* and cards on which you have written verb participles such as *going*, *falling*, *crying*, and *singing*. Have two students come forward and hold the *He* and *going* cards. Tell them that they must act very sad because they will not be able to go on their trip unless they become a complete sentence. But wait! (At this point, ringing a beautiful bell or tapping a triangle will be just perfect.) There is a helpful helping verb who is coming to their rescue! Of course, you know what happens next. Halo-adorned *is* glides into place between them, creating *He is going*, and all frowns turn to smiles. Repeat with *She* and *going*. Then change pace by having two students stand together and hold the *They* card. Of course, *is* cannot help here, so (ding! goes the beautiful bell) halo-bedecked *are* glides into place between them and the word *going*, and happiness returns. (See Figure 4–2.) Repeat with different verb participles—*falling, crying,* and *singing,* for example—and adjust the action of the verb accordingly.

Materials needed: cards, marker, props such as tinsel, glitter pens, bell, and cottas

She Said, He Said, They Said . . .

Said permeates students' writing, but when you think of all of the emotions that color human speech, it just seems so *blah.* Perhaps students use it because they don't have a ready resource of alternate words at hand. Have them scour their own writing, the current chapter in their pleasure reading books, the last chapter or short story from their literature study, the newspaper, or any other authentic piece of text to create a class list of words that authors use instead of *said.* Maintain a growing list of these for class reference. Not sure what the difference is between *He chortled* and *He laughed?* Aha. An authentic reason to visit the dictionary! Create a semantic map of these

FIG. 4–2 *The Helpful Helping Verb*

words according to their emotional connotation—*anger, fear, happiness, humor,* and so on.

Materials needed: current texts, students' writing, pleasure reading books, chart paper, marker

TV Comes to Life

Turn television into an ally rather than a foe. Identify several half-hour TV shows or cartoons that you find acceptable in terms of content. Give students a list of these and have them choose one to watch with a small notebook in hand. In that notebook, they record the actions portrayed by the main character or characters. The next day, they act out the verbs they saw and the rest of the class guesses the verbs and what show or cartoon they watched.

Materials needed: notebooks, pencils, TVs

How Shall I Say It?

Using the list your class created in She Said, He Said, They Said, write the alternative words for *said* on cards, one word per card, and have each group of four students select four cards. Students each identify a quotation from their writing in which they have used *said*. Each writer reads his quote in the voice that would be required by the verbs the group has chosen. For example: She cried, "Give it to me." She retorted, "Give it to me." She chuckled, "Give it to me." She whined, "Give it to me." Which of the verbs fits best with the author's context? None of them? Trade cards with a neighboring group and try again!

Materials needed: list from She Said, He Said, They Said activity, three-by-five-inch cards, marker, students' writing

Tense Codes

Don't change tenses! If it's in past tense, keep it in past tense! How many times have teachers uttered these admonitions? Granted, reading a piece that injudiciously changes tenses is close to hearing fingernails on a chalkboard. But sometimes the writer needs to change tenses in order to make the meaning clear. Consider this example:

> Brad is my favorite brother. We will be having a surprise birthday party for him tomorrow. I will have made him seven funny cards by the time his party starts. Last year I forgot his birthday and didn't make him any. I hope he forgets that I forgot.

Try that one for the *keep your tenses the same* rule! Present, future perfect, future perfect progressive, and past tenses all exist in harmony in the piece about Brad's party, and the reader hears no screechy fingernails when reading it. In Tense Codes, students underline the verbs in a piece of their writing. Above each, perhaps with an editorial blue pencil, they code the verbs. Younger children might use the codes *Pr, Pa,* and *Fut* for simple present, past, and future tenses. If you are studying more advanced verb tenses, simply adjust the codes for what you are studying. For example, *Pr Perf, Pa Perf,* and *Fut Perf* might be the codes if you are working on the perfect tenses. When students notice, as they will, that they have tense changes, have them consult with a response partner and decide together whether the tense change fits with the meaning in the piece or whether it alters the meaning. Through this process, tense shifts become purposeful meaning carriers rather than random errors. Of course, those tenses that have shifted injudiciously still will raise hackles and need to be changed.

Materials needed: students' writing, blue pencils

This Old Man and Helping Verbs

Our graduate assistant Kristi became caught up in our world of grammar. She located the following song idea on *www.lessonplanspage.com.* It's a variation of the old song "This Old Man." Students sing this tune, using the forms of helping verbs. Creativity is prized here as students are challenged to come up with rhyming lyrics for such things as

have, has, had

do, does, did

be, am, is, are, was, were, been

can, could, shall, should, will, would, may

might, must

Picture you and your class singing "This old man, he played have, he played knick-knack on my calf. With a knick-knack, paddy-wack, give a dog a bone, this old man came rolling home." Then, "This old man, he played has, he played knick-knack on my jazz. With a knick-knack, paddy-wack, give a dog a bone, this old man came rolling home," and so forth. Doesn't make sense? Who cares? Your students will be singing, and remembering, the forms of verbs.

Materials needed: none

Be *the Verb*

Every verb has a subject—someone or something that is doing or being it. In this activity, each student selects an action verb and writes it in its present-, past-, and future-tense forms (in marker so that all can see) on a five-by-eight-inch card with a string attached so that it can be placed around the neck. Keeping their verbs secret, students go home and assemble simple props or rudimentary costuming that would suggest the persona of the subject that would go with the verb. For the verb *crawled,* for example, a student would write *crawl, crawled,* and *will crawl* on her card. She might then bring in a baby bottle and a rattle, or even dress in a white piece of fabric folded to suggest a diaper. Each student then stands before the class while the class guesses the verb or verbs that might go with her garb. (See Figure 4–3.) When the class guesses the correct verb, the student puts the verb card around her neck. In this example, the class might guess *cry/cried/will cry*, *coo/cooed/will coo*, or *burp/burped/will burp*, or any other baby action. Great! Your goal is to get them thinking about verbs, so arriving at the correct one is merely a secondary issue.

Materials needed: five-by-eight-inch cards, markers, string, props

Charades

Action verbs were made for charades. Select action verbs from a current text, or have students submit favorite verbs from their writing. Write each verb on a slip of paper. The list might include *jumping, running, skipping, throwing, flying, tripping, sliding, diving, crying, laughing, spitting,* and so on. Each student selects a slip of paper and acts out the verb so that the rest of the class can guess it. (See Figure 4–4.) Adjust the difficulty and nuance of the verbs to the age of the students.

Materials needed: current texts, students' writing, slips of paper and pencils

FIG. 4–3 Be *the Verb*

FIG. 4–4   *Charades*

The Sounds of Photographs

Cut photographs from magazines and old calendars, or scour your personal collection for pictures that evoke thoughts of action. A picture of a waterfall might bring to mind *splashing, roaring, trickling,* and *falling*. A photograph of a storm might trigger *booming, cracking, crying,* and *slicing*. Give a photo to each pair of students and have them brainstorm all of the verbs suggested by the picture. Have them mount the photograph on construction paper and surround it with its verbs. Display these in the hallway or in the classroom.

Materials needed: old magazines, calendars, pictures, construction paper, scissors, markers, glue

Walking in Authors' Footprints: Verbs

Jerry Spinelli writes of the "kid drowning in his clothes" in *Maniac Magee* (1990, 85). Eve Bunting writes, "There are warehouses with windows blinded by dust and names paint-scrawled on their brick walls," (n.p.) and "The phone wires rocked the moon in their cradle of lines" (n.p.) in *Secret Place* (1996). *Drowning, blinded, paint-scrawled,* and *rocked.* What potent verbs! Katie Wood Ray (1999) paints a rich picture of a classroom that apprentices itself to such authors. Share these examples, and others you have located in the texts you use in your class, with your students. Have students look at each example and think of how the author *might* have said the same thing. What if Spinelli had said, "The kid's clothes were too big," or if Bunting had written, "There are dirty brick warehouses"? How would these versions compare? Which paints the most vivid word picture? Have volunteers share a sentence from their writing. Write the sentences on the board and, as a group, play with ways of inserting strong verbs.

Materials needed: authentic texts, chalkboard and chalk

Just Scream No to Boring Verbs—A Classroom Verb Thesaurus

Just say *no* to boring verbs. Have students choose a piece of writing from their folder and identify five verbs, like *say, go,* and *told,* that lack power. With a thesaurus and a partner, they identify stronger, more potent verbs to substitute for the weak verbs they originally used. Have them list the original verb and its options on paper. Assemble these into a classroom verb thesaurus for future use.

Materials needed: thesauri, students' writing, materials for making a class book, markers

Sportswriting

Sportswriters know the power of verbs. Somehow, the batter who *slammed* the ball over the wall seems like a better athlete than one who *hit* it over the wall, even though they both scored a home run. Using newspaper sports sections, *Sports Illustrated,* or other action-packed reports, have students circle powerful verbs associated with athletics. Create your own *Sportswriters' Guide to Strong Verbs* and make it available in the classroom writing center.

Materials needed: sports magazines, sports sections of newspapers, materials for making class book, markers

Comparative Sportswriting, Old Chap

The Internet places international newspapers at our fingertips. Have your students log on to any British newspaper and read the sports section. They will encounter not only verbs but also British idioms, in such phrases as *booked their place in the tournament* (earned a place), *scraped in* (barely made it), *top-scored for the team* (scored the most points), *being staged at* (being played at), *smashed* (beat), *turned the air blue* (cursed), and more. Your young athletes may enjoy creating a British English/ American English sports dictionary. A jolly good activity, don't you think, mate?

Materials needed: access to the Internet or British newspapers, materials for creating sports dictionary, markers

Conjugating the World Around Us

Many remember conjugating verbs with displeasure; running a verb through its tenses in meaningless sentences can be monotonous at best. Verb tenses are heavily taught in the upper-elementary and middle school grades—serendipitously, we think, at a time when children are at a very sociocentric stage of their lives. What others think and do is of paramount importance to these preadolescents as they measure themselves against others in their growing-up world. We think that verb conjugation and *what others do* are a great match for this level. To begin this activity, have students identify people they would like to know more about. Friends, family members, a favorite teacher or coach, members of the high school football team or cheerleading squad—noble candidates, all. Students choose a person and write a letter, prepare a phone-call script, or plan a face-to-face interview with their subject to ask him to name five action verbs that tell what he *does* in his life. Each student then conjugates the five verbs that she has discovered. It's still conjugation, but having an admired face attached to the sentences just might make it more bearable.

Eddie punts the ball.	Eddie kicks the ball.
Eddie punted the ball.	Eddie kicked the ball.
Eddie will punt the ball.	Eddie will kick the ball.
Eddie has punted the ball.	Eddie has kicked the ball.
Eddie had punted the ball.	Eddie had kicked the ball.
Eddie will have punted the ball.	Eddie will have kicked the ball.
Etc.	Etc.

Materials needed: paper and pencils

Comic Strip Speech Bubbles

Have students cut out their favorite comic strip from the newspaper and rewrite the speech bubbles, changing the tense. (See Figure 4–5.) Their challenge will be trying to maintain the humor while doing this. They might even need to add another frame to the comic strip or change the illustrations in some way. Correction fluid will come in quite handy in this activity! You can photocopy and enlarge the comic strips and hang them in your classroom.

Materials needed: comic strips, correction fluid, pens

Motion Gradient

Select a *tired verb* that your students overuse. Take, for example, *walked*. Draw a horizontal line on your chalkboard and write "slowest/least upbeat" on the left-hand side and "fastest/most upbeat" on the right-hand side. Divide students into pairs and have each consult a thesaurus to identify a word that is listed as an alternative for *walked*.

FIG. 4–5 *Comic Strip Speech Bubbles*

(Perhaps you will want to do this the day before the Motion Gradient activity will take place so that you can make sure you get a variety of words.) In this example, possibilities would include *stumbled, limped, hobbled, tiptoed, waddled, ambled, sauntered, padded, traversed, strode, cantered, promenaded, strutted, swaggered, reeled, trudged,* and *shuffled.* Have each pair write its word on a card and look in the dictionary to find the definition. When establishing the gradient, have each pair come to the board and place the card in the gradient relative to the other words already there. (See Figure 4–6.) As each pair comes forth, they obviously will have to make decisions and move some cards. Great! The point here is not to achieve the absolute gradient of slowest/least upbeat to fastest/most upbeat, but the conversation that ensues as students argue and defend their stances about the words.

Materials needed: cards, tape, thesauri, dictionary, markers

Cheerleading

Sports and cheerleading seem to come into play around fourth grade. Perhaps it is the sociocentric nature of this age, or perhaps it is the culture of the community, but team sports and those who lead the supportive fans seem to become a preoccupation at this age level. Our thought on this is carpe diem—seize the day! The same fervor that accompanies team sports can be transposed into service for verbs. Have students identify the verbs that reflect the pride that accompanies being part of a team— *go, fight, win, triumph, trounce, buffalo, hornswoggle, conquer, topple, obtain, prevail.* Stumped for words? Why, have your students consult the thesaurus, of course, and list these words on cards. Have students create and perform cheers that urge their favorite team to victory using the verbs they have identified.

Materials needed: thesaurus, cards, markers, paper and pencils

FIG. 4–6 *Motion Gradient*

Verb Jeopardy

Verb Jeopardy, a game that is adaptable to any part of speech, can help your students with their understandings of the types of verbs. Verb Jeopardy is played like the regular TV game show. Your students need only to come up with the correct questions for verbs you have chosen. (See Figure 4–7 for a sample Jeopardy board.) Once you have modeled this, students can have a good time creating their own Jeopardy games using verbs from their own writing and the texts in the class. Perhaps there will even be a tournament of champions in your class.

Materials needed: Jeopardy transparency or poster, authentic texts, students' writing

Tenses

In this game, which is played like old maid or authors, students attempt to make the most *books* in order to win. A book consists of the present, past, and future tenses and the infinitive form of a verb, and there are twelve books in a deck of Tense cards. You will need a deck of cards for each foursome of students. But what verbs should you use? Why, students can make their own cards using verbs from their writing or from the current class text, of course.

Divide your class into groups of four. Give each member of each group twelve Tense cards (or index cards). Each group member consults her writing folder or current text and identifies three interesting verbs. For each verb selected, she makes a

	Action Verbs	Verbs of Being	Transitive or Intransitive?	Does It Have Regular or Irregular Past Tense?
100	It means to make music with your voice.	It fits into this sentence: *She ___ going tomorrow.*	He *cried.*	To *call*
200	It means to cut wood.	It fits into this sentence: *He ___ run before I got there.*	She *carried* the bucket.	To *run*
300	It means to create a story on paper.	It fits into this sentence: *She ___ know better.*	They *walked* to the store.	To *pester*
400	It means to ride a horse at a fast speed.	It fits into this sentence: *He ___ gotten the letter by Tuesday.*	I *hope.*	To *bring*
500	It means to prepare for a test.	It fits into this sentence: *I ___ waiting for two hours.*	We *returned,* but did not like it there.	To *fantasize*

FIG. 4–7   *Verb Jeopardy*

card for the infinitive, present tense, past tense, and future tense (3 verbs × 4 tenses = 12 cards per person). For example, perhaps a student has written *With a burst of speed, I sprinted to the finish line* in her piece about winning the field day race. She might be especially proud that she used the vivid verb *sprinted* instead of the tired verb *ran*. The book for this verb would consist of four cards (*to sprint, sprint, sprinted, will sprint*). With each student contributing three books, the foursome will have created its own personalized deck of Tense cards. Use colored index cards, or white cards marked in color on the edges, so that each group's deck has a different color, or you will be driven crazy trying to sort them after each use.

To begin play, the dealer deals out all of the cards in the deck to himself and three other players. The person to the left of the dealer draws a card from the hand of the dealer and adds it to her hand. If it makes a book, she lays the book down and continues to play. If not, play continues as the person to her left draws a card from her hand, and so on. The winner is the person who lays down the most books. Groups can exchange their decks with other foursomes so that they are exposed to many more verbs.

As a variation, you may want to specify that the students use the current piece of literature, or the science text, or the newspaper. If your students are way beyond simple tenses, simply substitute the requirement that they use perfect, progressive, or perfect progressive tenses.

Materials needed: three-by-five-inch cards, markers, students' writing, current texts

The Yes-and-No Grammar Game

Roberta McManus uses the Yes-and-No Game to deepen students' understanding of concepts in her science classes with great success (Topping and McManus 2002b, 78). Based on the theory of concept attainment that suggests that concepts are best attained by looking at critical attributes and critical nonattributes, the Yes-and-No Game merely simplifies the terms into more kid-friendly language. On a T-chart, the teacher lists critical attributes of a concept under the heading "Yes" and the critical nonattributes under the heading "No." This game can be played with any two parts of speech, but it is especially potent when studying nouns and verbs. Try this:

YES	NO
bark	window
chair	desk
run	potato
fly	tv

By now, you may have guessed that words in the "Yes" column are words that can function as both nouns and verbs (the *bark* of a tree, the dogs *bark*) and that those in the "no" column function as only one part of speech. After listing about four words in each column, challenge the students *not* to name the concept, but to test their emerging idea of the concept by giving you exemplar words that would fit into one of the columns. You respond by placing the words they suggest in the appropriate column. (Other yeses in this case might be *finger*, *cry*, and *cough*; other nos might be *seek*, *rug*, and *poster*.) You will be amazed, by the way, at how difficult it is to think of words that fit the "No" column. Words in the English language are very versatile! A great word to include as a challenge in the "Yes" column is *candle*. It functions as a noun (light the *candle*), but it has a lesser-used function as a verb for chicken farmers (*candle* the egg). When you play this game throughout a day when you have a few minutes here and there, you just might find students running to the dictionary to check on alternative meanings for words they thought they knew (like *candle*).

Materials needed: chalkboard and chalk, dictionary

Tense Tents

On butcher paper, cut out three large tents—one to serve as the past-tense tent, a second for the present-tense tent, and a third for the future-tense tent. If your tense study is more sophisticated, simply substitute the tenses that are part of your curriculum. Students peruse newspaper headlines and magazine articles (or any other disposable text) and cut out verbs. They glue the verbs onto the appropriate tense tent, collage style.

Materials needed: butcher paper, newspapers and magazines, scissors, glue

What Happened?

Write this sentence on the board. *He _____ and the crowd screamed.* Have students brainstorm all of the verbs that could fit into that sentence. Students have schemata for sports, music, families, friends, pop stars, heroes, and a host of other experiences that can supply verbs for that sentence—*fell, tripped, scored, jumped, bowed, played, ran, smiled, won, laughed, cheated.* And, if their schemata fall short, they can consult a thesaurus and create a list of lesser-known verbs. Have pairs of students choose one of the verbs, find the nuances of its meaning in the dictionary if needed, and act it out for the class to guess. Add these words to your class' growing wall of words to consult when writing.

Materials needed: thesaurus, dictionary, chalkboard and chalk

In the Olden Days

Here is an interesting story. Today we call verbs such as *go/went/gone* irregular. Long ago, these verbs were considered to be the good guys. As a matter of fact, they were called *strong* verbs, while those verbs that merely added an inflected ending or helping verb were called *weak* verbs. Hmmm. Sounds like a call for dramatics, with half of the class playing the part of the strong verbs and the other half portraying the weak.

Of course, both sides have to pore over verb tenses in order to come up with verbs to portray—a teacher's review dream come true. In addition, they can be creative as they plan out ways in which they will act and speak and come up with improvised props or simple costuming they will use to depict their relative strength or weakness.

Materials needed: assorted props and/or simple costuming

Back to the Future

In Back to the Future, each student responds individually. The activity connects the abstractness of verb tense to authentic texts in the class. Give students index cards. On each, they write a verb tense that you have been studying (past, present, future, past perfect, for example). Read one sentence at a time from the current piece of literature or informational text. Their task is to listen for each verb and hold up the appropriate card to identify the tense being used. As a variation, a volunteer could read his current piece of writing one sentence at a time, with students responding by holding up the appropriate card. Being able to look at students' individual responses is an added bonus for you. At a glance, you will be able to tell who understands and who doesn't.

Materials needed: three-by-five-inch cards, current texts, students' writing

Verb Tenses, Mother Goose, and Art

Take present and future verb tenses, add Mother Goose and art, and you've got (pardon the colloquialism) a great activity. Match this up with a genre study you are doing in realistic fiction or science fiction and you will be triple-dipping into the old curriculum pot! We all know that Little Miss Muffet *sat* on her tuffet, eating her curds and whey, when along *came* a spider and *sat* down beside her and *frightened* Miss Muffet away. What if Ma Goose were writing today? Little Miss Muffet just might encounter not only present tense but also a beanbag chair, tofu and sprouts, and a mosquito infected with West Nile virus. *Little Miss Muffet is sitting on her beanbag chair, eating her tofu and sprouts, when along comes a West Nile virus mosquito and sits down beside her and frightens Miss Muffet away.* Your literature curriculum focuses on science fiction? Well, Miss Muffet *will sit* in her *spacecraft*, and so on. Take a familiar nursery rhyme, have your students write and illustrate it in present or future tense, and see what understandings develop about tense, genre, and art.

Materials needed: nursery rhymes, paper and pencils, markers

Quick Review of Subject-Verb Agreement for Teachers

A general rule: Singular subjects require singular verbs; plural subjects require plural verbs. *Ex. The man cooks. The men cook.*

Agreement with Person: Use the verb alone when writing in first or second person. *Ex. I run. You run.* Add -*s* to the verb when writing in third person. *Ex. He runs. She runs. It runs. Jane runs.*

Subject and verb need to agree even when there are intervening word groups between them. *Ex. The example taken from the tests is too hard. This type of assessment tool is authentic.*

Subject and verb need to agree even when the sentence is inverted (verb before the subject, as in a question). If you aren't certain, simply flip the sentence into a declarative sentence in your mind to check on agreement. *Ex. Are Judy and Kim in school today?* (Flipped) *Judy and Kim are in school today.*

Compound subjects joined by *and* take a plural verb. *Ex. Linda and Arlene are meeting us for lunch. Her mother and her teacher were at the luncheon.* Exception: If you are using two subjects to mean the same person, use a singular verb. *Ex. Her mother and teacher is the one who should get the award.* (Mother and teacher = same person.)

Indefinite pronouns such as *one, each, either, neither, everyone, everybody, anyone, anybody, someone, somebody, no one* and *nobody* are considered singular and take a singular verb. *Ex. Everyone who attended the party is talking about it. Each of the teachers has a set of keys.*

Some indefinite pronouns, such as *all, any, none, most, such* and *some,* do not clearly express singular or plural. Rely on the meaning of the rest of the sentence to tell which verb form to use.

Collective nouns like *audience, team, troupe, family, group, crew, gang,* and *faculty* take a singular verb if the group is considered a unit. If the group is considered as individuals, it takes a plural verb. *Ex. The faculty was in agreement. The faculty were leaving by twos.*

Some singular nouns end with -*s* but require a singular verb. Be careful with words such as *aeronautics, athletics, billiards, civics, economics, ethics, mathematics, measles, mumps,* and *the United States. Ex. Mumps is a childhood disease. Mathematics is his major.*

Literary titles and names of businesses are considered singular and require a singular verb. *Ex. Chaucer's* Canterbury Tales *is on school reading lists. Howard, Hood, and Schneider, Ltd. is a reputable business.*

Sums of money and measurement are considered singular when they are considered a unit, but plural when the elements are thought of individually. *Ex. Ten dollars was the price of the book. Ten dollars were thrown around the room.*

Some nouns, such as *glasses*, *pants*, *scissors*, *fireworks*, and *clothes*, are used only in their plural form, so they take a plural verb. *Ex. Her glasses are dirty. The fireworks were gorgeous.*

(Goldstein, Waugh, and Linsky 2004, 87–97; Brandon 2006, 102–4)

■ Playing with Subject-Verb Agreement

Super S Saves the Day Once Again

S is a facile little letter, serving verbs as well as nouns. You saw how Super S saved the day by making singular nouns plural in Chapter 3. He is just as useful with subject-verb agreement. Once again, you will need to designate one child as Super S and give him a card with the letter *s* on it (and, better yet, the old Superman cape with an S emblazoned on it). Weave a story about how lonely singular nouns are. They are so lonely that their verbs need to have company. And, who better to add for company than the mighty Super S! Plural subjects, on the other hand, already have company so they don't need Super S to help them out.

Prepare word cards for *The, boy, boys, people, run, child, children, jump, man, men, frown,* and other singular and plural nouns and basic verb forms that your students will recognize. Pass these out. Have the children holding *The, boy,* and *run* come forward. Tell the child holding *boy* to look very sad because he is alone (singular form). From the back of the room, have Super S call, "Don't worry! Here I come!" as she races to stand next to the verb *run* to make the sentence say *The boy runs.* Repeat with *The boys run.* Of course, in this sentence, there is no need for Super S because the boys will keep each other company. Our thanks to Brian for this great activity!

Materials needed: cards, marker, cape

Phone Book Search

Collect old phone books and use the yellow pages in this cut-and-paste activity for locating names of businesses that should function as a collective title. Have students create a class book of business advertisements and a thumbnail description of each, using the appropriate singular form of the verb. For example, *EZ Carpets is a business that will clean your carpets while you are at work and will guarantee that there will be no odors when you come home.*

Materials needed: old phone books, scissors, glue, paper, markers

■ English Language Learners and Verbs

Verbs in the English language have many different facets that pose difficulty even for native English speakers. Irregular verbs, in particular, are troublesome and make generalization about verb tenses confusing. These vagaries are further complicated for ELLs because verbs in their native languages may hold equally unique characteristics. Some of those differences are described in the following chart.

In Spanish, verbs indicate tense and number. Therefore, your ELL authors may write *Sylvia cans cook.*

In Navajo languages and in Mandarin Chinese, there are no verb tenses. Therefore, your ELL authors may not change verb tense when writing in what should be past and future tenses.

In Vietnamese, there is no verb *to be.* Therefore, your ELL authors may write *I fine* for *I am fine.* The system of tenses is different from English. Therefore, your ELL authors may write *I go yesterday* for *I went yesterday.* Subject-verb-object order is not used when speaking about weather, distance, or time. Therefore, your ELL authors may write *Is raining* for *It is raining outside.*

In Cantonese, helping verbs are not used for questions or negatives. Therefore, your ELL authors may write *How much this cost?* for *How much does this cost?*

In Korean and Japanese, the verb comes after the subject and object. Therefore, your ELL authors may write *The man the car drove.*

In Korean, there are no auxiliary verbs. The verb always is one word. Therefore, your ELL authors may write *Dan to school going-be.*

(Brandon 2006, 89; Haussamen 2003, 53–5; Swan and Smith 2001, 101, 315, 329)

Check It Out!

Identify the underlined verbs in the following piece of student writing by using these terms:

action verb
verb of being
present, past, or future tense
present perfect, past perfect, or future perfect tense
present progressive, past progressive, or future progressive tense
present perfect progressive, past perfect progressive, or future perfect progressive tense

1. Soccer **is** a game that **has been** popular all over the world. 2. It **is** comparatively recent that soccer **came** to the United States as a serious sport. 3. However, soccer **has not earned** the status of baseball, football, basketball and hockey. 4. Kids all over the country **are learning** how to dance with the ball. Youngsters are heading the ball and kicking it. 5. There **are** soccer teams and clubs all over. In addition, there are soccer Moms and soccer Dads. Soccer is played with eleven team members. 6. Each of the team members **runs** on the field except for the goalie. 7. The goalie's job **is** to make sure that the other team does not get the ball into the goal. The other team members all have special positions to play. 8. When the kids who **have been playing** soccer become adults, they **will want** to follow professional soccer rather than baseball. 9. These kids **will have been** involved in soccer and **will want** to watch it on T.V. the way their parents **watched** their favorite professional sports.

Answers to test available in Appendix F.

Admirable Adjectives and Adverbs

Those precious nouns, pronouns, and verbs that serve as the bases of sentences are beautiful things. But, as we know, even the most beautiful outfit can benefit from a bit of accessorizing, and that's just what adjectives and adverbs do. They accessorize—add layers of meaning to—the already quite lovely nouns and verbs. Just as the perfect scarf or a tie can make one's apparel *sing*, well-chosen adjectives and adverbs intensify the mental pictures we get from nouns and verbs.

You may be thinking, *Ah, yes, I remember liking adjectives and adverbs. They made writing "pretty." But, let me think. Adjectives describe things, right? And adverbs end in -ly. Is that all I need to know? What else do I need to tell my students?* Here to remind you is a quick review and some absolutely apt activities for your classroom.

Quick Review of Adjectives for Teachers

Adjectives: modify nouns and pronouns; answer the questions Which one? What kind? and How many? *Ex. The red Volvo is mine. Long dresses are my favorite. They have four children.*

> **Descriptive Adjectives: tell what kind.** *Ex. red Volvo, long dress*
> **Limiting Adjectives (also called determiners):** tell which one and how many.
>> Possessive: *my book, your apple*
>> Demonstrative: *this book, those books, that book*
>> Indefinite: *either book, any book, many books, some books*
>> Interrogative: *which/whose/what book*
>> Numerical: *one/two/three book/s*
>> Articles: *a book, the book, an apple*

Comparative and Superlative Forms: used for comparing two (comparative) or more than two (superlative) things.

> **One- or Two-Syllable Adjectives:** add *-er* or *-est*. *Ex. tall, taller, tallest*
> **Multisyllable Adjectives:** use *more* (comparative) or *most* (superlative).
>> *Ex. beautiful, more beautiful, most beautiful*
> **Irregular Comparatives and Superlatives:** use your writer's and reader's ear, and the dictionary, to help you with irregularly formed comparatives and superlatives. *Ex. good, better, best*

(Ellsworth and Higgins 2004, 2)

■ Playing with Adjectives

Adjective Books to Share

These fantastic books will make *your* students *hungry* to learn more about *admirable* and *able* adjectives.

Barrett, Judi. 1983. *A Snake Is Totally Tail.* New York: Atheneum.

Boynton, Sandra. 1983. *A Is for Angry: An Animal and Adjective Alphabet.* New York: Workman.

Cleary, Brian. P. 2000. *Hairy, Scary, Ordinary: What Is an Adjective?* Minneapolis: Carolrhoda.

Duke, Kate. 1983. *Guinea Pig ABC.* New York: Dutton.

Heinrichs, Ann. 2004. *Adjectives.* Chanhassen, MN: Child's World.

Heller, Ruth. 1989. *Many Luscious Lollipops: A Book About Adjectives.* New York: Grosset and Dunlap.

Hubbard, Woodleigh. 1990. *C Is for Curious: An ABC Book of Feelings.* San Francisco: Chronicle.

Maestro, Betsy. 1979. *On the Go: A Book of Adjectives.* Illustrated by Giulio Maestro. New York: Crown.

McMillan, B. 1989. *Super, Super, Superwords.* New York: Lothrop, Lee and Shepherd.

Big, Bigger, Biggest

The illustrations in *The Biggest Bear* (Ward 1952) match perfectly with the concept of positive, comparative, and superlative. Bear begins as a cute little cub occupying a tiny portion of the page. Then he grows big and bigger on succeeding pages until he is biggest of all, taking up the full illustration page. Share this book with your students. Have students fold a piece of paper in thirds vertically, then in half horizontally. This will result in spaces to practice the positive, comparative, and superlative forms of four different adjectives (two on the front of the page, two on the back). In the first row of three boxes, they draw *big, bigger,* and *biggest bear.* In the second row, change the adjective, perhaps to *fierce, fiercer,* and *fiercest cat,* and so on. Use adjectives and nouns that are appropriate to the age of your students. The details they choose to show the differences among the forms will be very interesting.

Materials needed: authentic text, paper, markers

Soft Toss

Soft Toss is an appropriate activity to use when you are studying the five senses. Use a colorful scarf knotted at one end, a small stuffed animal, or any other interesting soft items you can find. With students in a circle, toss the object to a child, who must then give you an adjective that describes how it looks, feels, smells, or sounds. (For obvious reasons, we have not included taste!) This child then tosses the item to another child, who must suggest a different adjective. Continue until the students experience difficulty thinking of more adjectives for the first item, then change to a different soft item and start again.

Materials needed: assorted soft items

Adjective Ferris Wheel

With students' desks arranged in a circle, have students write their names on a piece of paper and leave it on their desks. On a signal from you, they rotate clockwise like a big Ferris wheel, stopping at the next student's desk to write a *positive and respectful* adjective that describes that person. When you signal, they rotate again and again, each time reading the adjectives listed and adding another. Keep the Ferris wheel going as long as the students are being productive in generating different adjectives. When they return to their seat, they will love reading the adjectives that their classmates attributed to them.

Materials needed: paper and pencils

Artistic Adjectives

Give each student a sentence strip, on which she will write a descriptive adjective in large cursive or manuscript letters. Have students illustrate their adjective to make it look like what it describes (see Figure 5–1). They can add flourishes, faces, colors, and special effects with markers, glitter, stickers, or any media you have handy. Post these around your classroom or in the hall. Think of the possibilities for *fierce, frigid, stupendous, sweltering, gorgeous, disgusting, striped,* and many more!

Materials needed: sentence strips, markers, special-effects media, glue

Walking in Authors' Footsteps: Adjectives

You have only to look at the texts you use for shared reading and literature study to find a wellspring of adjectives. Katie Wood Ray (1999, 166–7, 170) notes the following:

▶ the use of *striking* adjectives, as in Jane Yolen's unconventional use of the word *drowned* in *Letting Swift River Go* (1992): "Then I heard my mother's voice coming to me over the drowned years" (n.p.)

▶ the use of adjectives *after a noun* instead of before, as in Libba Moore Gray's *My Mama Had a Dancing Heart* (1995): "drink lemonade cold" and "drink hot tea spiced" (n.p.)

▶ the use of *make-your-own* adjectives, as in Jerry Spinelli's *Maniac Magee* (1990): "That's why his front steps were the only un-sat-on front steps in town" (17), and

FIG. 5–1 *Artistic Adjectives*

in Robert Burleigh's *Home Run* (1998): "Then there is only the echoey, nothing-quite-like-it sound" (n.p.)

Your watchful eye, and those of your students, will notice a wonderful variety of adjectives once you begin to look. With your class, develop a list of ways in which authors use adjectives in interesting ways such as those Ray pointed out. The passages in the previous list would be a good starting place. Share them, one at a time, talking about what the author did. For each adjective use, share your writing and have students do the same to locate places where that technique would work and where it would not.

Materials needed: authentic texts, students' writing, teacher's writing, chart, paper, marker

Angry Adjectives Versus Namby-Pamby Nouns

Tell students that adjectives get very angry when they are pressed into service because nouns are too namby-pamby. (According to *Webster's New World Dictionary* [1988, 900], *namby-pamby* means "wishy-washy, without vigor.") In the sentence *She came across a big, big man*, the noun *man* is namby-pamby, and the adjective *big* is angry! Why should it have to work so hard when another noun like *giant* or *behemoth* would get the author's meaning across without the adjective's help? Challenge students to locate adjectives and the nouns they modify in their own writing. Then have them decide if the adjectives are necessary or if they are there simply because the nouns are too namby-pamby and in need of change. Create an ongoing chart of examples of angry adjectives and namby-pamby nouns and the noun substitutions that would be so much stronger.

Materials needed: chart paper, markers, students' writing

Alexander and the Terrible, Horrible, No Good, Very Bad Day

At one time or another, every child finds a soulmate in Judith Viorst's (1987) poor Alexander, who had a terrible, horrible, no good, very bad day. While it's true *She came across a giant* in the preceding example is better than *She came across a big, big man*, the same probably would not be true of Alexander's day. *Alexander and the Disaster? Alexander and the Calamities?* No, Viorst knew that the string of adjectives was just what she needed in order to show Alexander's accumulating annoyance with his day. *Alexander* is an opportunity to help students examine this aspect of Viorst's style. Share a piece of your writing in which a string of adjectives might help you emphasize a point. Have students help you revise it in Viorst's style, then have them look at their drafts to see if there are places where a string of adjectives would be effective in showing a growing feeling or mounting urgency. Ask for volunteers to share their original sentences on sentence strips so that the whole class can collaborate in trying out this interesting adjective use.

Materials needed: authentic text, sentence strips, teacher's writing, students' writing, markers

Parent Conference Prep

Shortly before parent conference time, have students prepare two lists for you to use when talking to their parents. They label the first list with the statement "Please describe me as a _____ girl/boy," and the second list with "Please don't describe me as a _____ girl/boy." Under each heading they list the adjectives they do and do not hope you use. You and the parents will enjoy sharing these on conference day!

Materials needed: paper and pencils

That [Blank] Noun

This activity is similar to the Motion Gradient activity described in Chapter 4. Write a sentence such as "The _____ chocolate cookies fell on the floor" and draw a line under the sentence, placing a minus sign (–) on the left end, a zero (0) in the middle, and a plus sign (+) on the right end. Give students three-by-five-inch cards on which they write an adjective that would fit in this sentence. Have them place their adjectives along a continuum from negative, to neutral, to positive connotation. Interesting discussion will ensue over such things as whether *three* is neutral in connotation or not. Is it more negative than *big*? Obviously, *disgusting* goes to the left end. But how about *stale*—is it more negative or more neutral than *disgusting*? Students will make many trips to the board to move their adjectives around as they argue and resolve the placements.

Materials needed: three-by-five-inch cards, pencils, tape, chalkboard and chalk

FIG. 5–2 *Stick Figures Evolve*

Stick Figures Evolve

Write "the _____ man" on the board and have each student draw a simple stick figure of a man. Add adjectives one at a time while they add details to their picture to match. (See Figure 5–2.)

old man   merry old man   cold, merry old man   brave, cold, merry old man

Materials needed: chalkboard and chalk, paper and markers

Greeting Card Images

Create a classroom collection of get-well, birthday, thank-you, and all-occasion cards that you and your students can use all year. Instead of throwing away the greeting cards you receive, bring them into your class. (Ask parents to do this, too.) Cut off the verse and signature, and use the front covers for a descriptive word activity. Pass them out and have students brainstorm a list of adjectives their scene or image evokes. Have the students mount the greeting card on a larger piece of folded heavy paper and write the adjectives all around it. Then, when someone in your school is sick, has a birthday, or needs to be thanked, your students will be ready to practice their social graces by sending a card.

Materials needed: old greeting cards, scissors, glue, heavy paper, markers

During your adjective study, play music in the background as your students come into the classroom. Vary the styles of music in terms of genre, time period, and mood. Write the name of the piece, the composer, and the approximate time period in which it was composed on a piece of chart paper, and have students list the adjectives that describe the piece. Elgar's *Pomp and Circumstance* might yield words such *stately* and *grand,* while Berlin's "God Bless America" might prompt *patriotic* and *proud.* Your music teacher colleague would be a good source of ideas and probably will thank you a million times over for contributing to music education, especially if you allow her to post the charts in the music room after they're finished. Our music teacher friend Jean provided us with a varied list of musical selections, which you can find in Appendix D.

Materials needed: selections of music, chart paper, markers

Missing Articles in the Newspaper

While it might sound strange, newspapers are notorious for lacking articles—in their headlines, that is. "Cards beat Cubs." "Link denied by sheriff." "Storm harms house." Of course, we all subconsciously insert articles so that the headline in our minds reads, "The Cards beat the Cubs." Obviously, newspapers omit articles, also known as limiting adjectives, in order to catch the reader's eye within space restrictions. Bring in newspapers and have your students cut out headlines and rewrite them, adding in articles (and other parts of speech) to make the headlines read as complete sentences. Talk about what is missing in headlines and why. As a change of pace, have them give newspaper-like titles to nonfiction pieces they have written or to chapters or sections in their informational texts.

Materials needed: newspapers, scissors, paper and pencils, students' writing

Vivacious Vocabulary

Bring your content area vocabulary together with descriptive adjectives and see what creative concoctions emerge. Brainstorm with your class to come up with as many interesting adjectives as there are students in the class (e.g., thirty students = thirty adjectives). As they suggest them, write them on three-by-five-inch cards. Place them facedown on a table and have each student choose one. Randomly pass out another set of three-by-five-inch cards on which you previously have written nouns from your current science, social studies, and math units. Each student's task is to put the adjective and noun together, think about what it would look like, and then draw it. What would a *rancid parallelogram* look like? A *bewitching butte? Humorous flotation?* This may sound like a silly activity, but you will be amazed at how much fun it is to review exact definitions of content area vocabulary and adjectives when you add a little art.

Materials needed: three-by-five-inch cards, current texts, paper and markers

Quick Review of Adverbs for Teachers

Adverbs modify verbs, adjectives, and other adverbs; they answer the questions How? Where? When? and Why?

Very often, adverbs are formed by adding *-ly* to adjectives. *Ex. He ran* quickly. Other types of adverbs are used to answer specific questions. *Ex.* Where? *He ran away.* When? *He ran yesterday.* Why? *He ran because of the race.* To what degree? *He ran as fast as he could.*

Adverbials: a phrase used to answer a question about a verb.
Ex. because of the race

Positive, Comparative, and Superlative Forms: formed by adding *-er* (comparative) and *-est* (superlative) or by adding the words *more* and *most*.
Ex. fast, faster, fastest; slow, more/less slow, most/least slow

Commonly Confused Adjectives and Adverbs: *good* and *well, bad* and *badly, real* and *really.* Some rules of thumb:
Always adjectives: *good, bad,* and *real;* always adverbs: *badly* and *really.*
Good and *bad* are both adjectives that are used after linking verbs.
Ex. This is bad. I feel good. (This refers to a general good feeling.)
Well and *badly* are used as adverbs and modify action verbs.
Ex. She sings badly. I feel well, thank you. (This refers to health.) He plays the sax well.
Real is always an adjective and *really* is always an adverb.
Ex. He played the sax really well. The real candidate stood up.

(Goldstein, Waugh, and Linsky 2004, 214–18)

▇ Playing with Adverbs

Adverb Books to Share

Your students will enjoy these books *immensely.* Read them *often.*

Cleary, Brian P. and Brian Gable. 2003. *Dearly, Nearly, Insincerely: What Is an Adverb?* Minneapolis: Learner.

Heinrichs, Ann. 2004. *Adverbs.* Chanhassen, MN: Child's World.

Heller, Ruth. 1991. *Up, Up, and Away: A Book About Adverbs.* New York: Grosset and Dunlap.

Walking in Authors' Footsteps: Adverbs

As with adjectives, you can find a number of striking adverbs by looking closely at authors' voices. Ray (1999) provides examples of unconventional adverb use in Jane

Yolen's *Miz Berlin Walks* (1997) and Michael Cadnum's *The Lost and Found House* (1997). Consider the following:

> I'd walk with Miz Berlin, side by side, step by step, waiting cotton-quiet till she cleared her throat. (Yolen 1997, n.p.)

> All night trucks rumble past. But I hardly really sleep. (Cadnum 1997, n.p.)

Have your class examine these sentences and locate the adverbs. How did these authors use adverbs, both conventionally and unconventionally? What effect did this have on the reader? Make a chart titled "Interesting Ways That Authors Use Adverbs," listing Yolen's and Cadnum's sentences on it. Tell students that they will be adding to this chart as they discover interesting adverb use in their pleasure reading books and in the texts you read in class.

Materials needed: authentic texts, chart paper, markers

Beating the Glad/Sad Syndrome

The classic answer to "How did the character feel?" so often is either *happy* or *sad*. We call this the *glad/sad* syndrome. Students may lack a ready storehouse of alternative words, so all positive feelings manifest themselves in the word *happy* and all negative ones in *sad*. Here is a way to combat the syndrome through the regular texts you and your class read. Tape several sheets of paper together to create two long, thin charts. At the top of one of the charts write "glad" with the ⌀ symbol (à la No Smoking sign) over the word. Do the same with the word *sad* at the top of the second chart. In other words, you are declaring that your classroom is a no *glad/sad* zone! As you discuss texts in your class, let the characters and situations give you opportunities to implant alternative *glad/sad* words. A sample conversation might sound like this:

T: How do you think Wilbur felt when Charlotte wove "Some Pig" into the web?

S: Happy.

T: Why?

S: Because Charlotte thought he was special.

T: Yes, I think he did feel happy. When someone is happy because someone else thinks he is special, we say he feels *proud*. Let's add the word *proud* to our list of "No Glad" words.

These two growing lists will be a ready resource for your young writers to use in describing actions and feelings in their writing.

Materials needed: chart paper, markers, current texts, students' writing

Not Just -ly

The statement "Adverbs end in *-ly* and modify verbs" is overly simplistic. A central understanding of adverbs lies with their function. Adverbs tell *how, when, where,*

and *why* as they modify *verbs*, *adjectives*, and other *adverbs*. Have students dedicate a page in their notes to adverbs. On this page they make a chart that can grow as the year of reading and writing progresses.

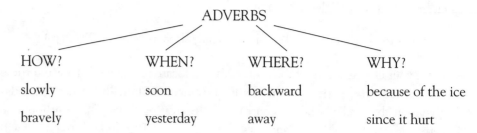

ADVERBS

HOW?	WHEN?	WHERE?	WHY?
slowly	soon	backward	because of the ice
bravely	yesterday	away	since it hurt

Materials needed: students' writing, authentic texts, students' notebooks, pencils

Clothesline

For this activity, you'll need to string a lightweight clothesline at eye level in your classroom and gather some lightweight clips or plastic clothespins. Have students select an adjective and an adverb from a piece of their writing (or from a current text) and write each on an index card. Prepare some simple subject and verb cards (for example, *The man, ran, The dogs, barked*). Attach a subject and a verb to the clothesline. Ask for volunteers to place their cards in the appropriate places on the line—adjectives before the noun, adverbs after the verb. See how many adjectives and adverbs can be added to the sentence and still make sense. As the sentence grows, you will have an opportunity to talk about commas and conjunctions, too, when students realize that *The funny nice chubby man ran quickly carefully* does not sound or look right.

Materials needed: clothesline, plastic clothespins or clips, cards, markers, current texts, students' writing

Pass the Cubes, Please

To help students remember the functions of adverbs, make an adverb cube and a verb cube from two square tissue boxes. Cover the boxes with green construction paper (green for action). On the verb cube, simply print "verb" on each of the six sides. On the adverb cube, print either "how," "when," "where," or "why" on each of the six sides, using two of them twice. Have students sit in a circle and pass the two cubes clockwise while you play music. When the music stops, the child holding the verb cube says a verb. The child holding the adverb cube flips it in the air. When it lands, he says an adverb that not only makes sense with the verb but also matches the adverb function indicated by the cube.

As a variation, add in two red cubes, one that says "noun" on each face and the other labeled with the functions of an adjective—"which one?" "what kind?" and "how many?" When the music stops, the holders of the red cubes state a noun and an adjective that would go with it, then the green cube holders do the same with a verb and an adverb. This version surely will keep students focused on the differences in meaning between adjectives and adverbs!

Materials needed: empty square tissue boxes, colored paper, glue, markers, music

Adverbs are words that *add* to the *verb*. Have each student identify a verb from his or her life. The soccer player might choose *kick*, the ballerina *dance*, and so forth. At the top of a piece of construction paper, each writes "I [verb]"—for example, "I sing." Beneath this, the student lists the types of words that would add to her verb and adds an illustration for each. For example:

I Sing.

How do I sing?	beautifully
Emotions?	joyfully
When do I sing?	daily
Where?	on the stage
Why?	because it is fun

See Figure 5–3.

Materials needed: construction paper, markers

FIG. 5–3 *Add to Your Verb*

Pick Up the Trash How?

Scatter some crumpled pieces of paper next to a trash can and tell students that you are going to have them perform a very simple task—picking up the trash. The catch is this: they must pick up the trash in very special ways. Assign one adverb to every two students. Their task is to look up the definition and brainstorm ideas for how they would pick up the trash in the way their adverb indicates. Think of the possibilities, for example, with the following adverbs and their definitions:

> defiantly—in an openly bold and resistant manner
>
> deferentially—in a courteous and respectful manner
>
> determinedly—in a resolved and decided manner
>
> discourteously—in a rude and impolite manner

Without dramatics, this is just a boring look-up-the-definition-of-these-adverbs exercise using the D section of the dictionary. With dramatics, you will find your students poring over a dictionary for a purpose and remembering new adverbs long enough to use them in their writing and speaking. Pair your shyer or less dramatic students with those for whom the world is a stage, and get ready for a lot of laughter—and learning.

Materials needed: trash can, crumpled paper, list of adverbs, dictionary

Adverb Ads

Have students create a "Job Wanted" advertisement, using adverbs to describe how they plan to perform the special skill they are marketing. Perhaps they will help with housecleaning. If so, their ad might say, "I work quickly. I dust completely. I run the vacuum cleaner thoroughly. Hire me now!"

Materials needed: paper and markers

■ English Language Learners, Adjectives, and Adverbs

Other languages differ in the placement of adjectives in the sentence and in how adjectives and adverbs are used. Like other parts of speech, adjectives and adverbs can confuse ELLs. For example, a native Spanish speaker who writes that someone is "the most funniest person" might be combining his newfound knowledge of English superlatives (add *-est*) with his native understanding of Spanish (add the word for *most*). A native Chinese speaker might have difficulty remembering to use articles in English because articles don't exist in her native language. The following chart describes some other examples.

In Spanish, adjectives can come after the noun. Therefore, your ELL authors may write *The bird red flew away.* Adjectives also can stand without a noun. Therefore, your ELL authors may write *I saw three prizes and I liked the small* instead of *I saw three prizes and I liked the small one.* In addition, comparatives and superlatives are expressed by the addition of *more* or *most.* Therefore, your ELL authors may write *I am more tall than my sister* or *Philadelphia is the most large city in Pennsylvania.*

In Russian, Polish, and Chinese, there are no articles. Therefore, your ELL authors may write *I see dog* or *I make pie.*

In Swahili, adjectives follow nouns. Therefore, your ELL authors may write *the day sunny.* Comparatives and superlatives are denoted by adding either *kuliko* or *kupita.* Therefore, your ELL authors may have difficulty remembering to add *-er* and *-est* to adjectives.

In Polish, adverbs sometimes are used in place of adjectives. Therefore, your ELL authors may write *The tree looks beautifully.*

(Swan and Smith 2001, 105, 155, 174–5, 272, 318)

Check It Out!

Use the following terms to identify the types of adjectives in the following piece of student writing:

possessive
demonstrative
indefinite
interrogative
numerical
limiting (article)
positive, comparative, superlative, or descriptive

1. Yesterday, I visited Ridley State Park in hopes of seeing some **neat** birds. 2. I would have been happy to see **any** neat birds. After a **five-minute** drive we reached the park. 3. As we walked along a **blocked-off** road, we saw a burned-out house. 4. **My** mother said that the old house had been burned down **one hundred twenty-five** years ago in a **blistering** forest fire. And then my Mother said, "Stop!" My eyes looked where her finger pointed. Twenty feet from us there stood an adult female deer. We watched the deer for five minutes straight without her ever being aware of us. Then on the trail of more grass she moved slowly away. We walked further down the road ever aware of the forest noises. My Mom stopped me again. 5. **This** time it was **an** immature green heron. Its beautiful plumage shone out from the dull bank. Its neck was green and its legs were yellow. Its long curving beak shone in the light. This great bird was a fisherman of sorts. It caught its prey by spearing it with its beak. I took a step closer in order to get a better view and I disrupted the heron. It took off and flew away in search of peace and quiet and more fish. 6. This was the **most** exciting experience.

Find the adverbs in this piece of student work.

The Revolutionary War

1. The great old bell tolled anew. 2. It pealed strongly for liberty, for justice, and for life. 3. And the people flocked around that great old bell and cheered. 4. And they sang loudly and they mourned silently.

Answers to test available in Appendix F.

Among Prepositions and Conjunctions and Interjections—Wow!

Imagine a piece of writing that contained rich nouns, pronouns, verbs, adjectives, and adverbs but left us wondering about how they all were related. How confused we would be! These major parts of speech, indeed, are potent, but they become actualized by seemingly small words that pack a lot of punch. These often underrated words are called prepositions, conjunctions, and interjections. They anchor us in a web of context that lets us know the critical relationships the author wants us to understand. Without them, we would be lost.

You may be thinking, *I remember something about prepositional phrases. Now, what was that? Conjunctions connect. Or, at least, I'm pretty sure they do. Interjections were those fun words. Right? Like* pow! *and* go! *I hope I can find ways to make them fun for my students.* Get ready for a visit to some small words that serve big purposes! Following brief reviews of prepositions, conjunctions, and interjections, you'll find ideas for bringing them to life for your students.

Quick Review of Prepositions for Teachers

Prepositions show the relationship between an object and other words in the sentence. They show how an object relates, or connects, with something else.

> *Ex. about, above, according to, across, after, against, along, among, around, as, as well as, at, because of, before, behind, below, beneath, beside, besides, between, beyond, but* (meaning except), *by, by way of, concerning, despite, down, during, except, for, from, in, in addition to, in back of, in case of, in front of, inside, in spite of, instead of, into, like, near, next to, of, off, on, onto, out, out of, outside, over, past, regarding, since, than, through, throughout, to, together with, toward, under, underneath, until, up, up to, upon, with, with reference to, with regard to, with the exception of, within, without*

Prepositional phrases begin with a preposition and end with a noun or pronoun that is called the object of the preposition.

> *Ex. Janet found the old newspapers inside the trash bag. JoAnne went to the airport. Louise laid the paper on the book.*

(Brandon 2006, 5)

Preposition Books to Share

You will want these books *in* your classroom *among* the other great books. Your students will read them *on* the floor, *upon* the rug, and *beside* their friends *during* free reading time.

> Berenstain, Stan, and Jan Berenstain. 1963. *Inside, Outside, Upside Down*. New York: Random House.
>
> ———. 1971. *Bears in the Night*. New York: Random House.
>
> Heinrichs, Ann. 2004. *Prepositions*. Chanhassen, MN: Child's World.
>
> Heller, Ruth. 1995. *Behind the Mask: A Book of Prepositions*. New York: Grosset and Dunlap.
>
> Hoban, Tana. 1973. *Over, Under, and Through and Other Spatial Concepts*. New York: Macmillan.
>
> ———. 1991. *All About Where*. New York: Greenwillow.
>
> Lillie, Patricia. 1993. *Everything Has a Place*. Illustrated by Nancy Tafuri. New York: Greenwillow.

Anything a Cat, a Troll, or Rosie the Hen Can Do

Students have a great deal of schemata for prepositions. If they have spent time watching a cat, or hearing the childhood favorites *The Three Billy Goats Gruff* (Galdone 1981) and *Rosie's Walk* (Hutchins 1971), they know that a cat never moves in a straight line and that story characters such as the trolls and Rosie the hen go *under, over, around, on,* and *beneath* all sorts of things. Capitalize on these schemata by having students act out the part of a cat, a troll, or Rosie the hen, moving among various simple objects in your room, and then list the appropriate prepositions. Turn this into an activity to share with younger buddies by having your students prepare to read one of these books aloud and guide the little ones in dramatizing it. They can make simple props out of construction paper (a green piece for the yard, a blue piece for the pond, two brown pieces for the fence, and so forth) or use a low bench or balance beam for a bridge, and their little friends can act out the prepositions you provide.

Materials needed: authentic texts, chart paper, simple props, construction paper, scissors, markers

Authors' Best Prepositional Phrases

Have your students search through the piece of literature currently under study or their own writing to find the best prepositional phrases. What constitutes the best? Perhaps it's the one that conjures up the richest image, or the funniest, or one that

spoke to them in some way. Part of the interest in this activity will be listening to their reasons for evaluating certain phrases as *best*. Post these around your room on sentence strips or on a chart.

Materials needed: current texts, students' writing, sentence strips or chart paper, markers

Preposition Poem

As its name suggests, a preposition poem is simply a poem in which every line begins with a preposition. Get triple curriculum duty from this poetry format by having students write about a current content area topic. Here is an example of a preposition poem about metamorphosis.

Here I Come!

Within my bed
On the branch
Until it's time
In a little space
With a lot of moving
Out of the chrysalis I come
Up in the air
Across the yard I fly!

Materials needed: paper and pencils

Preposition Proposition

Hide a gift certificate for "an extra ten minutes of free-time activity today for the whole class" somewhere in your classroom. Tell students that they can receive your special gift if they can follow your preposition proposition. On a transparency, write clues using prepositions and reveal them one at a time. For example, "in the classroom," "over a height of six inches," "by something white," "against something solid," and so on. (Select a volunteer to do the searching for the whole class to avoid a melee.) Have students create and decorate a gift certificate for someone important to them (for an extra hug, a big smile, or any nonmonetary gift of kindness) and a set of at least five Preposition Proposition clues leading to the place at home where they will hide it. Teachers often stress random acts of kindness and gifts of oneself at holidays and other special occasions. Here's a way to connect that to grammar.

Materials needed: transparency, overhead projector, gift certificate, paper and markers

In My Room

Have students draw a detailed picture of their bedroom (or any room in their home). If you are concerned about your students' living arrangements, have them draw your classroom or any other room in your school. After the drawing is complete, students write a description of the room, starting each sentence with a prepositional phrase, such as *In the corner, on the bed, over the doorway, inside the closet,* or *behind the lamp.*

Materials needed: paper and markers

Prep-a-Doodle

One of our students found a copy of this song, contributed by Corrie Napier on *www.lessonplanspage.com,* and shared it with us. Sing the following list of prepositions to the tune of "Yankee Doodle," and you just might find, as we did, that your class wants to challenge the class next door to a Prep-a-Doodle sing-off!

> About, above, across, after,
> Along, among, around, at,
> Before, beside, between, against,
> Within, without, beneath, through.
> During, under, in, into,
> Over, of, off, to, toward,
> Up, on, near, for, from, except,
> By, with, behind, below, down.

Materials needed: copies of song

Over the River and Through the Woods

Combine singing, women's history, and some preposition work in this activity. Many of us have sung "Over the River and Through the Woods" at Thanksgiving time, but how many of us know its origin? According to Jone Johnson Lewis (2005), author Lydia Maria Child originally published this poem in 1884 in her book *Flowers for Children, Vol. 2.* Child, who went by the name Maria, was one of the earliest American women to make a living as a writer. She wrote domestic advice books, a novel depicting pioneer life that was sympathetic to the Native American plight, and anti-slavery books and tracts. For her stand on the latter, sadly, many of her loyal readers turned away from her. "Over the River" remains well known, is a joy to sing, and serves as a ready-made preposition activity to use at Thanksgiving time. Just look at the prepositions your students can locate as they sing it over and over. Make sure they underline them all.

> Over the river and thru the wood,
> To grandfather's house we go;
> The horse knows the way
> To carry the sleigh,
> Thru the white and drifted snow, oh!
> Over the river and thru the wood,
> Oh, how the wind does blow!
> It stings the toes,
> And bites the nose,

As over the ground we go.
Over the river and thru the wood,
To have a first-rate play;
Oh, hear the bell ring,
"Ting-a-ling-ling!"
Hurrah for Thanksgiving Day-ay!
Over the river and thru the wood,
Trot fast my dapple gray!
Spring over the ground,
Like a hunting hound!
For this is Thanksgiving Day.
Over the river and thru the wood,
And straight thru the barnyard gate,
We seem to go extremely slow.
It is so hard to wait!
Over the river and thru the wood,
Now grandmother's cap I spy!
Hurrah for the fun! Is the pudding done?
Hurrah for the pumpkin pie!

Materials needed: copies of song, pencils

 Dear Doctor Science

The website *WebEnglishTeacher.com* included the following letter to Doctor Science and his reply. Both are humorous looks at the overuse of prepositions and can provide some comic relief in your day. Place them on a transparency and share them with your class. Ask them what they notice about Dr. Science's response. Underline his preposition "misuse" and talk about why they think he wrote it this way. This is a good time to introduce tongue-in-cheek humor, and some of your students might even be encouraged to try their hand at grammar humor with other so-called writing taboos.

Dear Doctor Science,
Is there a reason for not ending a sentence with a preposition that you can think of?

—John Mostrom from Seattle, WA

I must admit I don't know where you're coming from. Correct usage in English and Science is something I've devoted my whole life to. Of course, if I say anything you can't understand, it will just become a new hammer you can try to hit me or another expert over the head with. There are plenty of people like you I can't hope to change the mind of. But then, I've dealt with people like you before. People who don't really want to learn, but just hope to find someone they can publicly disagree with. There's little I can say that your type won't find something to object to. But getting back to your question, no, there's really no reason for not ending a sentence with a preposition, at least none I can think of.
—Ask Dr. Science
2002/05/30

Materials needed: Dr. Science letter on a transparency, marker

Conjunctions connect words, clauses, or phrases in sentences and show the relationship between or among them.

Types of Conjunctions

Coordinating Conjunctions: join parallel (or equal) words or groups of words—a noun with a noun, a verb with a verb, an adjective with an adjective, a main clause with a main clause, a subordinating clause with a subordinating clause, or a phrase with a phrase.

> *Ex. for, and, nor, but, or, yet, so. Katy spoke English and Spanish. Elmo can eat some spices but he cannot eat garlic. The intelligent yet humble Jerome accepted the accolade.*

Subordinating Conjunctions: link dependent clauses with independent clauses.

> *Ex. after, although, as, as if, as long as, as soon as, as though, because, before, but that, even if, even though, if, in order that, notwithstanding, provided, since, so that, than, that, till, though, unless, until, when, whenever, where, whereas, wherever, and while.*

> *Ex. Although Dora was bruised* (dependent clause), *she was not in pain* (independent clause). *If Louis wants to get an A* (dependent clause), *he will have to study very hard* (independent clause).

Correlative Conjunctions: occur in pairs and join parallel structures.

> *Ex. both/and, either/or, neither/nor, not only/but also, whether/or. Neither Shaniqua nor Laquisha is in a sorority. Alston not only played basketball but also played first base in baseball. Either Jerry will catch a fish or he will tell a fish story.*

(Goldstein, Waugh, and Linsky 2004, 220–21)

■ Playing with Conjunctions

Conjunction and Interjection Books to Share

Neither you *nor* your colleagues will be able to keep your students from asking for *both* read-aloud *and* read-alone time with these books.

Heinrichs, Ann. 2004. *Conjunctions*. Chanhassen, MN: Child's World.

Heller, Ruth. 1998. *Fantastic! Wow! And Unreal! A Book About Interjections and Conjunctions*. New York: Penguin.

Walking in Authors' Footprints: Conjunctions

Do not start a sentence with *and*, or so we were told by our English teachers. While this holds true much of the time, authors sometimes begin sentences with *and* to great effect. For example, Ray (1999) notes its powerful impact as a craft tool when used in the last sentence of a book. Even without knowing the rest of the story, it's hard not to feel the potency in these final lines:

And then a big wind came and set everything free. (Rylant 1992, 89).

And that was always enough. (Rylant 1982, n.p.)

And so I can remember, too. (MacLachlan 1995, n.p.)

Jane Yolen creates a sense of vastness by stringing together a list with *and*s rather than commas in *Welcome to the Green House* (1993): "there will be no more green house, not for the monkeys and fish and birds and bees and beetles and wild pigs and bats and kinka-jous and all the hundreds of thousands of flowers and fruits and trees" (n.p.). Our sense of urgency is piqued! While *and* can be anathema to a reader when it is not used well, it has tremendous power when used sparingly in the right places. When you are studying conjunctions and talking about the *general* inadvisability of starting sentences with *and*, be sure to share Rylant's, MacLachlan's, and Yolen's examples. Talk with students about why these seemingly rule-breaking uses are highly effective. Under what circumstances might this work? Invite students to share places in their writing where this craft technique might work, and do the same with your writing. Encourage students to bring unconventional uses of *and*—and other conjunctions—to the class' attention when they find them in their pleasure reading books.

Materials needed: authentic texts, teacher's writing, students' writing

Two or More Ands?

And probably is the most overworked conjunction in children's writing. Unlike Rylant, MacLachlan, and Yolen, however, children often don't overwork it for effect. It appears in run-on sentences in the guise of *and then . . . and then . . . and she . . . and I . . .* Have students check each of the sentences in a piece of writing to see if they have used two or more *and*s. If so, they might (but not always) need to revise. If they have a two-*and* situation in their writing, tell them to mark the sentence with an asterisk so they can ask you for help during their next writing conference.

Materials needed: students' writing, pencils

Hula Hoop-de-Doo

Prepositions and conjunctions can be confusing because they indicate somewhat amorphous relationships among nouns and verbs. To engage students in thinking about the functions of these parts of speech, place on the floor four hula hoops labeled "verb," "preposition," "noun," and "conjunction." On cards, write at least ten words that are examples of each part of speech. Distribute the word cards, and have students sit on the floor and place the words in the appropriate hula hoops. Discuss students' placement of the words. Invariably, the discussion will lead students to examine the intention of each part of speech. The discussion will be so much richer than just memorizing the definitions.

Materials needed: four hula hoops, cards, markers

A White Bus

Jane Kiester shares this activity in her book *Caught 'ya Again* (1993). A WHITE BUS is an acronym for the subordinating conjunctions:

A—after, although, as, as if, as long as, as soon as, as though

W—when, whenever, where, whereas, wherever, while

H—how

I—if, in order that

T—than, that, till, though

E—even if, even though

B—because, before, but that

U—unless, until

S—since, so that

Of course, this begs an artistic rendering. Give students white drawing paper, on which they draw and cut out a large white bus. On the side of the bus where it normally might say something like "The Fillstall Area School District," have students write "A WHITE BUS" in large, well-spaced letters. Beneath each letter, they can record the subordinating conjunctions. By the way, how many White Bus conjunctions are on page 43 of their current pleasure reading book? You might want to have them check to see.

Materials needed: white drawing paper, markers, scissors, current pleasure reading books

Counting the Fanboys

FANBOYS is an acronym for the coordinating conjunctions *for, and, nor, but, or, yet,* and *so.* Have students list the FANBOYS at the top of a piece of paper and open any text to page 13 (or any other page you suggest). On that page, they count the incidence of each of the FANBOYS conjunctions, using tally marks to keep track. Which conjunction(s) appeared the most? Was the frequency of certain conjunctions in certain texts higher than in others? Why might that be?

Materials needed: current texts, paper and markers

Shakespeare Said

In *Hamlet*, Polonius advised his son, "Neither a borrower nor a lender be." Clearly, Shakespeare knew about correlative conjunctions, among his other gifts. Someone

else (we're not sure who, but it sounds a lot like our fathers) gave us the adage "Either fish or cut bait." Reinforce the parallel structure of often misused correlative conjunctions by challenging your students to create their own adages based on the prompts "Neither _____ nor _____ be" and "Either _____ or _____." You will be surprised at the wisdom of your young students, and if you have them write and illustrate their adages, you can bind the sayings into a class book of collective advice to be passed down over the years.

Materials needed: paper, markers, materials for making a class book

Quick Review of Interjections for Teachers

Interjections enliven writing by showing strong feeling or emotion. Interjections do not have a grammatical connection with the rest of the sentence, and they often stand alone. *Ex. Oh, Whew! Yikes! No! Awesome! Wow!*

Mild Interjections: mild emotion; followed by a comma at the beginning of a sentence. *Ex. Oh, that's so sweet.*

Strong Interjections: more forceful feeling or emotion; usually followed by an exclamation mark. *Ex. Wow! That was a great show.*

(Brandon 2006, 7–8; Loberger and Welsh 2002, 137–38)

■ Playing with Interjections

Interjection Book for Children

Too much! Read! Now!

Heinrichs, Ann. 2004. *Interjections*. Chanhassen, MN: Child's World.

Interjection Connection

What kinds of interjections do authors use? This activity will help students answer that question. Using the current chapter they are reading in their pleasure reading book, have students make a list of the interjections they find. Have them note the kind of feeling the author was trying to get across as well.

Materials needed: pleasure reading books, paper and pencils

Interjection Overkill

Zowie! Interjections are fun. Cool! Oh, they really pack a punch in writing. Awesome! Egad! Once aware of them, though, young writers often overuse them, as we have done here. Bummer! To demonstrate that interjections are best used sparingly, have students take a piece of their writing or a page from a class text and insert an interjection at the end of *every* sentence. Read these aloud and watch the realization dawn that *more* is not necessarily *better*. (We would end this with "Aha!" but that would be overkill.)

Materials needed: students' writing, current text, pencils

Interjecting Storytelling

Storytelling can be an exciting collaborative activity, especially when the tellers have some help with their ideas. Assemble assorted small props, enough for every child to have one. (Most of us can do a quick sweep of our desks and come up with paper clips, a pen, a picture, a bell, a plant, and so forth. There is no right or wrong set of objects.) In addition, write enough interjections on three-by-five-inch cards so that each student receives one. Have students sit in groups of four and assign each a number, one to four. Give each child a prop and an interjection card. Child number one begins to tell a story that includes both his prop and his interjection. Upon a signal from you, child number two picks up the story and incorporates both her prop and her interjection. This continues until all four students in each group have had a turn. Ask for groups to volunteer to share their storytelling with the entire class.

Materials needed: box of props, three-by-five-inch cards, marker

Class Compendium of Comical Interjections

Comic strips are rich repositories of interjections. Because of the economy of space, "Thud!" is more appropriate, not to mention funnier, than "Then he hit the ground really hard." Have students scan newspapers for comics that include interjections, cut them out, underline the interjections, and contribute them to a class book.

Materials needed: comic strips, scissors, markers, materials to make a class book

TV Interjections

Within any half-hour sitcom or cartoon, how many interjections do the characters say? Have your students watch TV with a notebook in hand in which they record the interjections they hear. Share and discuss them in class.

Materials needed: notebooks, pencils, TVs

■ English Language Learners, Prepositions, Conjunctions, and Interjections

Even native English speakers have difficulty choosing the appropriate preposition from time to time. For example, think about the nuances of meaning among *standing in line, in the line, on line,* and *on the line.* For ELL students, this is compounded by preposition use in their native languages. Keep these differences in mind when you work with your students.

In Spanish, there is not the fine distinction among the prepositions *in/on/into, to/at/in, as/like, for/by,* and *during/for* that there is in English. Therefore, your ELL authors may write *Peggy has a part at the play* instead of *Peggy has a part in the play.*

In Greek, most prepositions have English equivalents, but not all of them. Therefore, your ELL authors may use some prepositions very well and then suddenly appear to be completely confused. The word *that* tends to replace *what.* Therefore, your ELL authors may write *Chucky did not remember that Hilda said to him.*

In Portuguese, there are fewer prepositions than in English, especially in relation to time, location, and movement. Problems occur when a Portuguese preposition has more than one English equivalent. Therefore, your ELL authors may write *Greg walked until the station* because the same word is used for both time (*until*) and distance (*as far as*) in Portuguese. *Like* and *as* are also represented by the same word. Therefore, your ELL authors may write *Sharman looks as a model.*

In Farsi, *and* is a widely used conjunction, particularly in the beginning of a sentence, and it often is used to connect strings of clauses. Therefore, your ELL students may start sentences with *and* and write run-on sentences.

In Japanese, conjunctions do not always have a one-to-one equivalence with English conjunctions. For example, *and* corresponds to eleven different Japanese forms. Therefore, your ELL authors may find English conjunctions very confusing.

(Swan and Smith 2001, 108, 125–6, 140–1, 151, 191, 224, 306)

Check It Out!

Identify the prepositions, conjunctions, and interjections in the following excerpt from a student's report about Russia. Use the following terms:

preposition
prepositional phrase
coordinating conjunction
subordinating conjunction
correlative conjunction
mild interjection
strong interjection

1. Russia has been invaded many times, sometimes successfully and sometimes not. 2. Here are some of the major invasions and their outcomes . . . . 3. Genghis Khan was a Mongol from Asia who attacked Russia in about the year 1200. 4. He overran the country and a generation later his grandson formed the Golden Horde which lasted until the year 1480 . . . . 5. Napoleon tried to conquer Russia with the largest army assembled until that time. 6. Although he reached Moscow (his troops severely ravaged the city), he was driven back by the severe Russian winter and the Russian troops . . . . 7. Hitler also failed to conquer Russia although at one point he controlled the Ukraine (a fertile area where most of the Russian produce comes from) and had subdued most of Leningrad. 8. Like Napoleon, his troops were forced to withdraw with the coming of the Russian winter. 9. Both the severe winter and the fierce Russian army defeated Hitler's army. 10. Oh! What a great loss of life.

Putting It All Together

While it's fun to explore types of sentences, clauses, and the separate parts of speech, the power of language is in experiencing it as a whole. What interesting things authors have to tell us! And what interesting things we can write so that others can read our thoughts! So, in this chapter, we offer activities that engage your students in looking at all of the parts as a whole. We hope that by now you are thinking, *I'm feeling more comfortable with grammar, and I'm ready for some ideas for putting it all together for my students. Oh (interjection), wow (interjection)! I (pronoun) need (verb) this (adjective) next (adjective) section (noun).* And, hopefully, it won't disappoint!

■ Playing with Grammar

Grammar Books to Share

Enjoy these books with your students. They include all of the parts of speech and are fun to read.

> Cleary, Brian P., and Brian Gable. 2004. *Pitch and Throw, Grasp and Know: What Is a Synonym?* Minneapolis: Carolrhoda.

> Maizels, Jennie, and Petty, Kate. 1996. *The Amazing Pop-up Grammar Book.* New York: Dutton.

The Adventures of Thesaurus Rex

Laya Steinberg's *Thesaurus Rex* (2003) is not only a delightful story but also a treasure trove of parts of speech. Lovable Thesaurus Rex starts his day "stretching, reaching, extending, bending." Then, "Uh oh! His pants need mending." Throughout this relatively short and funny book, verb tenses change, interjections pop up, pronouns refer to Rex—in other words, it's a great little book for having your students identify parts of speech. Young children enjoy it for the story; older ones will enjoy it, too, especially if they can say, "Oh, we're identifying parts of speech," if someone catches them enjoying it as much as any six-year-old!

Materials needed: authentic text

Grammar Wizard of the Day

Assemble any or all of these props—a pointed hat, a robe, an oversized Harry Potter–esque pair of glasses, a wand—and you will be ready to bestow the honor of being the Grammar Wizard of the Day upon one of your students. Each day one student dons the garb you've assembled and presents a sentence from a current piece of writing to the rest of the class, pointing out its parts of speech, the type of sentence, or whatever you have studied so far. (See Figure 7–1.) Have students sign up for their day ahead of time so they have time to prepare. Of course, this will require them to apply all that you have been teaching them and to ask you questions about anything that is puzzling. They can write their sentence on a transparency, chalkboard, whiteboard, or any other kind of technology you regularly use. This is a quick two- to three-minute presentation that you can include as part of your daily opening routine.

Materials needed: students' writing, wizard props, chalkboard and chalk

FIG. 7–1 *Grammar Wizard*

Calisthenic Parts of Speech

When the snow or rain has rendered outdoor activities useless, take heart. This activity will get your students moving and having fun, and they won't even realize that it's really a grammar review. Have them help you decide on a particular action to perform for each part of speech. For example, *verb* might be running in place, *noun* might be standing at attention, *adverb* might be pumping their arms in the air quickly. The particular action really isn't important as long as they agree on it. List the parts of speech and the associated actions on the board for reference. Read a sentence aloud from one of their texts twice. The first time, they just listen. The second time, read it slowly as they act out the part of speech that each word represents. Afraid that they won't be able to identify all of the parts of speech quickly enough? Then discuss this before the second reading. Remember, this is not a test. You're trying to teach and reinforce here.

Materials needed: current text, chalkboard and chalk

Musical Chairs—Where Nobody's Out

This is a variation on the old musical chairs activity. Give each student a card on which you have written a part of speech and line up enough chairs for everyone in your class, minus one. Play music while students walk around the chairs. When the music stops, everyone attempts to sit in a chair. The person left standing says her part of speech and a word that is an example of it. Unlike the old party game, however, do not remove a chair. Keep playing so that a different person with a different part of speech will be the one left standing the next time you stop the music.

Materials needed: chairs, cards, marker, music

Meet the Grammar Family

Create life-size people by tracing around some of your students as they lie on pieces of butcher paper. Cut these out; you will need one for each part of speech you teach. Introduce the cutouts as the Grammar family and have students help you name them. Some suggestions: Norma Noun, Vincente Verb, Adelia Adjective, Ashante Adverb, Priscilla and Pablo Pronoun (holding hands so you can elicit masculine, feminine, and plural pronouns in the activity), Conrad Conjunction, Penny Preposition, and Inez Interjection. As you introduce each part of speech, have students label appropriate words on the family member. For Norma Noun, for example, labeling her *head, hand, leg, foot,* and so on would be obvious choices, as would *clothing* words and *jewelry* words. Vincente Verb might have *kick* on his foot, *wink* on his eye, and *snap* on his finger. Adelia Adjective might have *muscular* on her upper arm and *blue* on her eye. You get the idea! Display the Grammar family and add more words to them as time goes by.

Materials needed: butcher paper, scissors, glue, crayons or markers

Color-Coded Drafts

If your students keep early drafts of pieces they've written in their writing folders, have them select one and color-code the parts of speech you have studied so far. Using crayons or highlighters, they simply color lightly over the words. They can create a legend (nouns = red, verbs = green, adjectives = blue) that suits them, perhaps even delving into the creative colors available today in highlighters and crayon boxes.

Materials needed: multicolored highlighters or crayons, students' writing

Revisiting Schoolhouse Rock!

Students who have grown up with public television will recognize the parts-of-speech songs contained in the *Schoolhouse Rock!* videotape, *Grammar Rock* (Warburton 1973/1997). With titles such as "Unpack Your Adjectives" and "Lolly, Lolly, Lolly, Get Your Adverbs Here," these songs are likely to bring a smile to your students' faces. Public television is not on the TV bill of fare in every home, though, so we recommend using this video in your classroom as you introduce each part of speech. Students can sing along, illustrate the songs, or act them out with their own interpretations.

Materials needed: video, TV, VCR

Parsing Knock Knocks

Although most adults don't care for knock-knock jokes, young folks do. And they tell them over and over and over until we want to scream. Since these jokes are not likely to go away, use them to serve a higher purpose. Tell students you will listen to their knock-knock jokes if they write them down and tell you the parts of speech they contain. For example:

> Knock, knock. (verb, verb)
> Who's there? (pronoun/verb, adverb)
> Boo. (noun)
> Boo who? (noun, pronoun)
> Why are you crying? (adverb, helping verb, pronoun, verb)

Second graders in particular seem to love knock-knock jokes, so think about the possibilities of your older students writing and sharing knock-knock jokes with a second-grade class. Of course, you will need to see that they have identified the parts of speech correctly before they head off to share the jokes with their little friends.

Materials needed: paper and pencils

Grammar Outdoors

This activity is made for those days when you simply must be outdoors—the first balmy spring day, an unseasonably warm fall day, or a day when your classroom thermometer tops ninety degrees. Find a comfortable place to sit outside and invite your students to pick up an object—a stone, twig, blade of grass, leaf, ant, lost button—that is lying within arm's reach. Have them examine the object and list words, by part of speech, that they might use to write about it. Then have them use those words to write the kinds of clauses and/or sentences you have been discussing in class. Grammar practice in the fresh air, accompanied by a nice walk, might be just the break you need.

Materials needed: outdoor objects, paper and pencils

Shaving Cream

When the desktops are dirty, it's time for shaving cream. Not only will it clean the desks, but it also will give your class an opportunity to play with words. Squirt a bit of shaving cream on the children's desks. Have them spread it out to make a surface on which they can write with one finger. Give them words to write in the shaving cream, then have them vary the word forms. An example:

> Write the adjective *slow*. Add an ending to make it *comparative*. Change the ending to make it *superlative*. Now, change the ending so that it becomes an *adverb*. Add a *verb* in front of this word. Now, make that verb *past tense*. Now make it *future tense*. And so forth.

This activity works with any part of speech or parts of a sentence. (Example: Write a *dependent clause*; now add something to it to make it *independent*.) A word of caution, though: Use unscented shaving cream or you will send your asthmatics to the nurse's office for the rest of the day.

Materials needed: unscented shaving cream, paper towels for cleanup

Quilts and/or Local Art

In our area, quilting is a local art form. When we visit local schools, we regularly see quilts hanging in hallways and classrooms that depict scenes from stories, history, scientific discoveries, and more. We think that quilts could easily show the evolution of grammatical understandings over the course of a school year as well. When you study a part of speech or any other aspect of grammar, have your students illustrate it with fabric pens on a square of fabric. Have groups of students keep making new squares as the year goes by. At the end of the year, assemble the class quilt. Sew the squares together and back the result with cotton batting plus a solid piece of fabric to finish it off. (If you are not handy with a needle and thread and don't know anyone who is, you can accomplish the same thing by using squares of paper.) Display the quilt for all to see. Quilting is not your thing? Well, what is the indigenous art form in your area? Could it be pressed into the service of grammar? Ask your art teacher colleague. He'll be sure to have a suggestion or two.

Materials needed: fabric, scissors, fabric pens, needle and thread, cotton batting (or paper, markers, and tape)

Splashing the Unit Vocabulary

Although this appears to be a grammar activity, it really does double duty as a review of the concepts of your current content area study unit. Give students a legal-size piece of paper, preferably blue, to keep with the notion of a splash, or allow them to personalize the page with sketches of splashing water. Holding the paper horizontally, they fold it in half vertically, then in half again, thus making eight columns (four on one side of the paper, four on the back). They label each column with one of the eight parts of speech. Working in small groups, they *splash* as many unit-related words as they can under each part of speech. You will be amazed at how creative they get when they put their heads together to operationalize the unit concepts. For example, for a unit on Westward expansion words might be *brave* (adjective), *cautiously* (adverb), *they* (pronoun), *over* (preposition), *Help!* (interjection). The conversation that ensues will provide a review you'll love.

Materials needed: legal-size paper (preferably blue), markers, content area texts

Treasure Hunt

There is no shortage of environmental print in schools. The hallway bulletin boards, direction signs, notices, even the lavatories are alive with communication. Have students go, in pairs, on a Treasure Hunt to locate parts of speech in their school environment. Rather than turning them loose en masse, give each pair a specific area to peruse (Mrs. Marley's bulletin board, frontdoor notice, lavatory signs, etc.) and a time limit. You may need to *plant* some print so that the hunt is fruitful, so check the areas first. Each pair sets out with a notebook in which they try to record at least two (adjust for the amount of print available) examples of each part of speech. Compare the treasures they have found. What is the least common part of speech? The most common? Why?

Materials needed: environmental print, notebooks and pencils

The Carousel Walk

Turn a unit review or a literature summary into an opportunity for movement with a Carousel Walk. Post eight pieces of chart paper around your room, one for each part of speech, and divide your class into eight groups. Each group begins at a chart and writes words representing that part of speech that they associate with the unit or the story. They continue to brainstorm until you tell them it's time to rotate clockwise to the next chart. At each new chart, they read the words that have been listed and add more. If they disagree about the accuracy of content or the appropriateness of a word, they mark it with a question mark. Discuss and clarify any questionable words when they have rotated through all of the charts.

Materials needed: chart paper, markers, timer

Uncombine and Recombine

Display a sentence from one of your texts, cut apart into its individual words, in a pocket chart. With students sitting in a circle on the floor, have a student begin to

pass the first word around the circle as you play music. When the music stops, the child holding the word tells its part of speech. If correct, she keeps the word. If not, the word continues to circulate. Continue with the rest of the words in the sentence. At the end, have the students holding the words return them to the pocket chart to recombine them into the sentence.

Materials needed: pocket chart, sentence strips, marker, scissors, music, current text

Erase This!

Divide the class into two teams. Each team develops a list of words that represent each of the eight parts of speech, using their current pleasure reading books as resources. Assign each team to a portion of the chalkboard on which they write these words in a random fashion (so that all of the nouns, verbs, and so on aren't together). Line up the two teams behind a piece of tape on the floor so that they are facing the opposite team's portion of the board. Say, "Erase this: a conjunction," and the first person on each team runs to the board to erase a conjunction placed there by the opposite team. The first to erase correctly and return to the starting mark gets a point. Continue with other parts of speech until all of the words have been erased. In order to even the playing field, so to speak, give each team some time before the race begins to problem solve any words they are not sure about. This may even involve using a dictionary and its references to parts of speech. Now, isn't that a tricky way to get them using that resource?

Materials needed: pleasure reading books, chalkboard and chalk, erasers, dictionary, tape

Crossword Puzzles

Key "crossword puzzles" into any Internet search engine and you will find multiple sites that will help you and your students create crossword puzzles with a minimum of keystrokes. Select a site that makes you comfortable and share it with your students. Show them a crossword puzzle book (for example, any of the *New York Times* crossword puzzle books). Challenge them to create a class crossword puzzle book that you will then copy and make available to them. Tell them they can use the vocabulary words associated with any unit of study, current or past, but their clues must include the part of speech as well as the definition. Are they allowed to look in the glossary of their content area texts? Absolutely! Turn them loose and watch the level of excitement (not to mention review) rise. Crossword puzzles provide the kind of language involvement that keeps the mind sharp. Who knows? Maybe you will be starting a lifelong crossword habit in your students. So much better than leisure time devoted to TV viewing.

Materials needed: access to the Internet, sample crossword puzzle books, content area texts, materials for making a class book

Henny Penny

Teachers of emergent literacy use pattern books such as *Henny Penny* (Galdone 1984) to develop their little ones' sight vocabulary because these books are predictable and simple. We think these beloved books have a place in the upper grades as well. Revisit *Henny Penny* when you are beginning to get students to look at how parts of speech come together in sentences. The simplicity and repetitive structure will provide opportunities for ample reinforcement as well as a chance for students to walk down memory lane. After reading the book out loud, write one sentence from it on a transparency. Model how you identify and label the parts of speech. Write a second sentence and guide your students in identifying and labeling. When you feel that they have a grasp of the activity, write further sentences from the book and have them practice together, then alone. Need more book suggestions? Ask your kindergarten and first-grade teacher colleagues for ideas.

Materials needed: authentic text, transparency, overhead projector, markers, paper and pencils

Diamantes

Diamantes not only sound delightful but also look neat when written in their diamond shape. The formula for creating them involves close consideration of parts of speech:

> 1 word (a noun, subject)
> 2 words (adjectives describing noun in line 1)
> 3 words (*-ing* or *-ed* verb participles that relate to line 1)
> 4 words (first two nouns relate to line 1; second two nouns relate to line 7)
> 3 words (*-ing* or *-ed* verb participles that relate to line 7)
> 2 words (adjectives describing line 7)
> 1 word (a noun, opposite of line 1)

When you combine this formula with oppositional concepts from your content area unit, you get deeper thinking about the concepts because *every word* must be carefully chosen. Here is an example from social studies that juxtaposes slavery and freedom:

> Slavery
> horrible unfair
> crying wanting picking
> owners masters railroad hope
> running hiding praying
> welcome beautiful
> Freedom

Materials needed: transparency or chart with formula, paper and pencils

You Can Find It in Our Library

Have your students categorize titles in your classroom library by parts of speech. Prepositional phrases? *The Trumpet of the Swan* (White 1970), *When I Was Young in the Mountains* (Rylant 1982). Adjectives? *The Revenge of the Incredible Dr. Rancid and His Youthful Assistant, Jeffrey* (Conford 1980), *Nappy Hair* (Herron 1997). Proper nouns? *Maniac Magee* (Spinelli 1990), *Stuart Little* (White 1974). Some titles are complete sentences, like *What's Alice Up To?* (Jessup 1997) and *My Mama Had a Dancing Heart* (Gray 1995), and some are dependent clauses, like *If You're Not from the Prairie* (Bouchard 1995). Still others defy conventional rules, like *Me and Caleb Again* (Meyer 1969), and offer opportunities to discuss why authors use their license to break the rules. The titles in your classroom library contain a rich resource for whatever you are studying. A side bonus is that this activity gets students browsing through books. Who knows what will happen when a title intrigues them or they hear another student gasp, "Oh, I loved that book!"

Materials needed: library books, paper and pencils

Dear Old Ivan Capp

IVAN CAPP is an acronym for the parts of speech (interjection, verb, adverb, noun, conjunction, adjective, preposition, pronoun). But what does he look like? Encourage your students to be creative by drawing what they think he looks like. Clearly, he should be doing (verb) something (noun) exciting (interjection) in a special way (adverb) with a certain look (adjective) in relation (preposition, conjunction) to something else who/that (pronoun) has some kind of a reaction!

Materials needed: paper and markers

Good Songs, Bad Grammar

Although it may be painful to our ears, we really should listen closely to the lyrics in the music our students love. Some of the content is questionable, but more to the point of this book, some of the grammar is atrocious. You'll hear aberrations of almost everything you know about correct usage. The truth is, they are going to listen to it no matter what you think, so we say, let's find a way to use it. Many CDs come with an insert containing lyrics; if not, you'll just have to listen closely. Choose a school-appropriate song or verse that just begs for correct usage and copy it onto a transparency or chart. (You will really pique their interest if you play the song while you ceremoniously unveil the lyrics.) Instead of defaming the lyricist for his poor grammar (which probably is what the students will expect you to do), use this as an opportunity to talk about multiple discourses that mature speakers and writers know how to use. The lyricist undoubtedly knew how to write in formal English but chose nonstandard usage because this is a pop song in which she wanted to convey emotion, protest, or a musical pattern. How might she have written the song in formal English? As a class, try rewriting the lyrics in formal English and singing them! You might find it useful to surround this activity with a proposition: Suppose the principal invited this recording artist to sing for a school assembly but only if she rewrote the lyrics to conform with formal grammar. What would the song sound like?

Materials needed: teacher-selected songs, transparencies, marker, overhead projector, paper and pencils

Jabberwocky

The creative mind of Lewis Carroll gave us the fanciful "Jabberwocky" in *Through the Looking-Glass and What Alice Found There* (1872). With only a passing glance, one might be inclined to pass Carroll's invention off as nonsense. On closer grammatical inspection, however, meaning begins to emerge. Challenge your students to help you decode this piece by parsing it for its parts of speech and sentence constructions. Here is an example.

'Twas		brillig,	and		the	slithy	toves
pronoun/verb of being		verb*	conjunction		article	adjective	noun

Did	gyre	and		gimble	in		the	wabe
Verb	verb	conjunction		verb	preposition		article	noun

*Depending upon the context, *brillig* could be a verb ('Twas snowing), an adjective ('Twas huge), or a noun ('Twas summer).

You just might find that you have creative minds in your classroom that can use "Jabberwocky" as a model for creating their own version. Lewis Carroll would be proud, indeed.

Materials needed: transparency of "Jabberwocky," overhead projector, markers

Why Is It Funny?

William Safire's *Fumblerules* (1990) has brought chuckles to even the most seriously studious language aficionados. Share these chapter titles from this funny little book and ask students why the statements are funny:

No sentence fragments. (1)

Avoid run-on sentences they are hard to read. (4)

The adverb always follows the verb. (16)

Reserve the apostrophe for it's proper use and omit it when its not needed. (28)

Write all adverbial forms correct. (31)

In their writing, everyone should make sure that pronouns agree with its antecedent. (34)

When a dependent clause precedes an independent clause put a comma after the dependent clause. (46)

If any word is improper at the end of a sentence, a linking verb is. (52)

Verbs has to agree with their subjects. (58)

And don't start a sentence with a conjunction. (67)

The passive voice should never be used. (70)

Writing carefully, dangling participles must be avoided. (72)

Resist new verb forms that have snuck into the language. (103)

Better to walk through the shadow of the valley of death than to string prepositional phrases. (106)

One will not have needed the future perfect tense in one's entire life. (112)

Place pronouns as close as possible, especially in long sentences of ten or more words, to their antecedents. (115)

Remember to never split an infinitive. (121)

Don't verb nouns. (127)

Never use prepositions to end sentences with. (145)

Materials needed: transparency of fumblerules, overhead projector, marker

Twinning Languages

When speakers of two languages get together, they often ask each other, "How do you say _____ in your language?" Take this natural curiosity and extend it into an activity in which you pair a native English speaker and an English-as-a-second-language speaker to look at how parts of speech and syntax play out in the two languages. Present a simple sentence in both languages. For example:

> *I live in a blue house* (English) compared with *Vivo en una casa azul* (Spanish): In English, the adjective comes before the noun; in Spanish, it comes after.

> *Are you going to school?* (English) compared with *¿Vas a la escuela?* (Spanish): In English, the verb of being *are* is used. In Spanish, *vas* means *you go* and there is no need for a verb of being. In addition, questions in Spanish begin with an inverted question mark.

> *I don't know anything* (English) compared with *Yo no se nada* (Spanish): Spanish uses the double negative, whereas English does not.

If you're not multilingual, ask for help from the students, the ESL teacher in your building, the high school foreign language department, parents, and community members. Have the students discuss, compare, and contrast how the two languages appear to work.

Materials needed: paper and pencils

This activity borrows from a review activity developed by Roberta McManus (Topping and McManus 2002b). Using index cards, prepare the playing cards for this game according to the following directions. You will notice that parts of speech are written in red, definitions in green, and example words in blue. (The definition on the front of each card does not match the part of speech on the back, but don't worry. That is intentional.)

card 1—(front is blank); (back, in red marker) *noun*

card 2—(front, in green marker) *a word used to name something—a person, place or thing*; (back, in red marker) *interjection*

card 3—(front, in green marker) *a word or phrase used to express strong emotion, usually set off by , or !*; (back, in red marker) *verb*

card 4—(front, in green marker) *a word that shows action or being*; (back, in red marker) *preposition*

card 5—(front, in green marker) *a word that shows the relationship between an object and other words in the sentence*; (back, in red marker) *adjective*

card 6—(front, in green marker) *a word that describes a noun or pronoun*; (back, in red marker) *pronoun*

card 7—(front, in green marker) *a word used in place of a noun*; (back, in red marker) *conjunction*

card 8—(front, in green marker) *a word used to connect words and groups of words*; (back, in red marker) *adverb*

card 9—(front, in green marker) *a word that modifies a verb, and tells how, when, where, why, how often, or how much*; (back is blank)

In addition to these nine cards you will need thirty to forty cards on which you write, in blue marker, words that exhibit each part of speech. You will gain extra mileage out of this activity by using current vocabulary, but following are some sample words that will serve the purpose: *was, because, from, his, weakly, greasy-haired, pilot, are, with, I, you, it, but, Benjamin Franklin, when, run, nicest, drink, to, the, or, Boo!, Good job!, yet, No way!, thinner, who, England, fear, sandwich, immediately, loudly, outdoor, and, nor, between, at, over, beside, Italian, move, the, expensive, up, streaked.* This activity works best when students are able to talk among themselves and problem solve, so randomly pass out all of the cards to pairs or small groups. Ask for someone to bring the red *Noun* card to the front of the room. Ask students to look at their green cards to see if they have the definition of a noun. The student with the noun definition comes forward. Having thus defined what a noun is, students next look at their blue cards and decide which, if any, of them fit the definition of a noun and bring those words forward. As a class, cross-check each example card with the definition to see if it is a match. Encourage best guesses and trial attempts. When the noun discussion is complete, have the holders of the word *Noun* and the noun examples sit down. The holder of the noun definition turns his card over to reveal the next part of speech, *Interjection*. Have the holder of the definition card, then the holders of examples, come forward. Play continues in this manner through the rest of the parts of speech.

The beauty of this game is in its conversation about words. For example, the holder of *Italian* might come forward as an example of a noun (as in *I am an Italian*). You then can say to her, "Oh! You are going to be busy today. I think you will decide to come forward again!" knowing that *Italian* also can function as an adjective. *Pilot* (as in *airplane pilot*, *pilot a plane*, and *pilot light*) is a similarly interesting word. When students make an incorrect suggestion, such as bringing forward *outdoor* as an example of a noun (saying, for example, "We play outdoors"), simply add another blue word card with the correct form. ("Oh, I see what you are thinking. You are thinking of the word *outdoors*. Great! That would be the noun form of that word. Let me make that card for you. Hold on to *outdoor* without the *s*, though, because I think you'll be bringing it up here again later on.")

Materials needed: prepared cards, colored markers, extra blank cards

The Dreaded (or Beloved) Diagramming

People learn in many different ways, so it is not surprising that some of us hated sentence diagramming and some of us loved it. For some, perhaps, it was an unnecessary layer of complication; for others, it was just the visualization they needed. Unfortunately, in many English classrooms it dominated as though diagramming were one of Maslow's basic needs, right after food, water, and shelter. Our view of diagramming is that it is a means to an end, with the end being the understanding of how sentences work. Developed in the late nineteenth century by Alonzo Reed and Brainerd Kellogg, two grammar teachers at the Brooklyn Collegiate and Polytechnic Institute, diagramming uses horizontal, vertical, and diagonal lines to show the relationship among words in a sentence. We consider it an art activity because it is visual. With the option of adding a bit of color or embellishment, some of your students may find that painting a sentence picture helps everything make sense. Sometimes, just the diagram of the core sentence is a revelation to a youngster. Using simple sentences, here's how diagramming works:

The basic *subject/predicate diagram* consists of a horizontal line bisected by a perpendicular line.

Dori jumped.

The *subject/predicate/direct object diagram* adds another perpendicular line that does not bisect the horizontal.

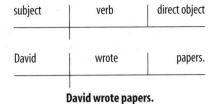

David wrote papers.

The diagram for the *subject/verb/complement* incorporates a diagonal line that leans toward the noun to which it refers.

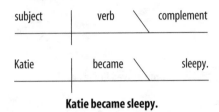

Katie became sleepy.

Indicate an *indirect object* by placing an extra horizontal line below the core sentence, attaching it with a diagonal backslash.

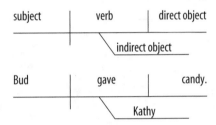

Bud gave Kathy candy.

Modifiers appear on backslash diagonals beneath the words that they modify.

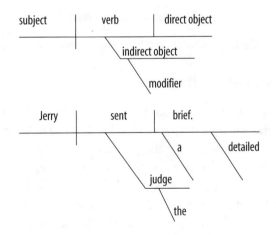

Jerry sent the judge a detailed brief.

Place *prepositions* on diagonal lines under the words that they modify. Place the *object of the preposition* on a horizontal line attached to this diagonal.

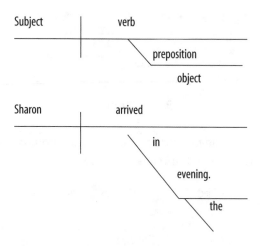

Sharon arrived in the evening.

Show *coordinating conjunctions* by using dashed lines that connect parallel words.

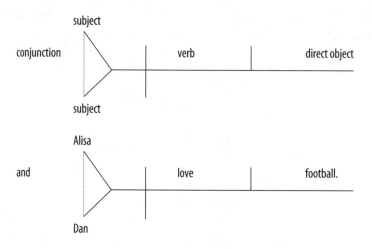

Alisa and Dan love football.

Materials needed: transparencies, overhead projector, markers, paper and pencils

The Human Sentence Diagram

This activity is similar to the Dreaded (or Beloved) Diagramming activity, but students act out the sentence diagram instead of drawing it. Write the component parts of a sentence on sentence strips and pass them out. Have the two students holding the simple subject and the simple verb come forward and sit cross-legged on a tabletop, holding their words in front of them. The holder of the direct object joins them next, followed by the indirect object, who positions himself below the verb. Then, students with the additional adjectives, adverbs, and prepositions join the diagram one by one, holding their words on the slant in the appropriate places. In the simple sentence *The Phillies won the game*, one student would hold *Phillies*, another *won*, and a third *game*. Two other students would join them, holding their articles, *The* and *the*, on the diagonal. (See Figure 7–2.)

Materials needed: sentence strips, marker

Song Lyrics

Encourage your students to bring in their favorite school-appropriate CD lyric inserts, and use them for practice in identifying parts of speech. Each student can select her own musical preference and use it as a personalized set of practice exercises.

Materials needed: student-selected lyrics, paper and pencils

Quick Review of Easily Confused Words for Teachers

adapt/adopt: *Adapt* means to change or alter; *adopt* means to take as your own.

affect/effect: *Affect* and *effect* are confusing because they can be used as both verbs and nouns and because they have a similar meaning of "something or someone doing or showing something to someone or themselves." Clear as mud, right? Here are the differences: *Affect* (verb) means to influence, as in "The weather affects Emma's arthritis by making her knees sore"; *affect* (noun) means the nuance of one's behavior or attitude, as in "She responded with a flat affect." *Effect* (verb) means to cause something to happen, as in "Pat effected a positive change by restructuring the committees"; *effect* (noun) means the result of an action, as in "The effect of Barbara's pronouncement will be felt for years."

FIG. 7–2 *The Human Sentence Diagram*

aisle/isle: *Aisle* is the walkway between rows of seats; isle is short for *island*.

already/all ready: *Already* is an adverb meaning before or prior to a specific time; *all ready* is an adjective meaning completely ready. It can be used in place of *ready*.

alright/all right: *Alright* is not an acceptable word; *all right* is an adjective meaning correct or acceptable.

among/between: Use *among* for more than two; *between* for only two.

can/may: *Can* connotes ability to do something; *may* connotes permission to do something.

disinterested/uninterested: *Disinterested* means impartial; *uninterested* means having no concern or interest.

everyday/every day: *Everyday* means ordinary; *every day* means each day in succession.

ill/sick: *Ill* means not well; *sick* means nauseated.

imply/infer: The writer or speaker *implies* what he is saying; the reader or listener *infers* what she reads or hears.

lay/lie: *Lay* means to put or to place; *lie* means to rest or to recline. Some of the words are the same in different tenses, which makes this pair especially confusing.

lay   laid   have laid
lie   lay   have lain

In days gone by, *lie* was considered a strong verb (*lie, lay, lain*), while *lay* was considered weak (*lay, laid, laid*). The current tendency to use *laid* as an all-purpose form for both *lie* and *lay* is an example of weak verbs surpassing the strong as the language evolves. However, *layed* is not correct anywhere, any time.

number/amount: *Number* refers to objects that can be counted; *amount* refers to things in bulk or mass.

raise/rise: *Raise* means to lift; *rise* means to ascend or to come up.

set/sit: *Set* means to put or to place; *sit* means to rest.

teach/learn: *Teach* means to impart the knowledge; *learn* means to acquire the knowledge.

then/than: *Then* indicates what comes next; *than* is used for comparisons.

(Loberger and Welsh 2002, 291–344; Brandon 2006, 184–88; Haussamen 2000, 61)

Mother, Can I? Mother, May I?

We both still remember saying to our mothers, "Can I go to the park?" and having our mothers respond, "Yes, you *can* go to the park but, no, you *may* not." Parents have their children's best interest at heart, and many a mother has corrected her children's usage of *can* and *may* with the same response. Maybe it's programmed into their DNA like "If everyone else jumped off the roof, would you?" but child-birth seems to bring particular clarity to the *can/may* dilemma. We say, "Why wait?" This activity will get students up and moving as they act out verbs *only* when they have received permission. Permission is granted when they use the correct form of *may*. Have students stand in a circle. Appoint one child to stand in the center of the circle and act as the parent. Have the other children ask questions in the format of "Mother [Father], can I walk [substitute any action verb]?" and "Mother [Father], may I _____?" To the *can* questions, the parent responds, "Yes, you *can*, but no, you *may* not." To the *may* questions, the parent replies, "Why, yes dear, you *may!*" Students are permitted to perform the action only when they have asked a *may* question.

Materials needed: none

Each Teach

Many teachers marvel at students' ability to explain things to each other when the teachers' best efforts have failed. This activity capitalizes on that student-to-student wavelength. Write pairs of easily confused words on cards and distribute them to pairs of students. Have students work together to plan a brief minilesson explaining the difference between the two words to present as part of the daily opening routine.

Materials needed: cards, marker, paper and pencils

Things You Can and Cannot Do

Frequently confused words almost beg to become a student-created book for your classroom library. Imagine the humorous illustrations that could accompany examples such as these: *You can adopt a cat, but you cannot adapt a cat. You can walk between two people, but you cannot walk among two people. You can stick your tongue in a light socket, but you may not stick your tongue in a light socket.*

Materials needed: paper, markers, materials for making a class book

Word Stories

Word stories tap into creative parts of our minds to create mnemonic devices that will help us remember things that we normally wouldn't be able to remember. They

add a layer of meaning. The best word stories are those that your children will create and share with each other. Following are a few examples:

adapt/adopt—If you ad*A*pt something, you ch*A*nge it. If you ad*O*pt something, you *O*wn it. (Match the vowels.) You wouldn't want to adapt a dog, would you? What would you change it into?

aisle/isle—An *A*isle shows the w*A*y.

among/between—Bet*w*een has *tw*in letters, *ee*, and should always be used for only twins, that is *two* people or things. "Bet*w*in the twins."

everyday/every day—Before using one of these forms, mentally substitute *each* for *every*. If *each* fits the context, use *every day*—two separate words. (You wouldn't write *eachday* as one word, would you?)

Materials needed: pencil and paper

Usage Sketches

Drawing may be just the channel some students need in order to clarify easily confused words. Have students fold a page in half and illustrate the following pairs of sentences, one on each side of the fold:

I *adopted* a puppy. I *adapted* a puppy. (Get ready for a funny drawing here.)

I will *lie* in my bed. I will *lay* a book on the bed.

She walked down the *aisle*. She walked on the *isle*.

Robin was *between* us. Robin was *among* us.

I will *raise* the flag. I will *rise*.

Materials needed: paper and markers or crayons

Editor's Nightmare Collage

What kind of artwork would give an editor nightmares? Why, a collage of usage errors, of course! Sadly, we don't have to look far to find errors in the environmental print that surrounds us. Have your students sharpen their editorial eyes and scan newspapers, church bulletins, restaurant place mats, signs, billboards, and so forth, looking for usage errors. Have them collect, photograph, or cut out these assaults on language and create a collage. Because they really do not wish sleepless nights on the editors of the world, they can create another collage that mirrors the first—this one with examples of correct usage.

Materials needed: poster board, environmental print, photographs, glue, scissors

Other People's Bloopers

If your email inbox is like ours, you probably find periodic blooper lists that your friends so generously forward to you. Many of these sayings are funny *only* because the writer dangled a participle or misplaced a modifier. So, instead of hitting the Delete key the next time a list arrives, save or print it instead. At least some of them will be appropriate for sharing, laughing at, discussing, illustrating, or dramatizing with your students. For example, a picture of *Walking through the forest, a tree fell on Michael's foot* might reveal a tree with big feet tripping over poor Michael. Facial expressions and body language will be hard to disguise when you act out the difference between *You nearly won a million dollars in the lottery* and *You won nearly a million dollars in the lottery* (Loberger and Welsh 2002, 102). Here are some other possibilities from anonymous sources that we've saved over the years:

The sick man went to the doctor with a high fever.

The patient lives at home with his mother, father, and pet turtle, who is presently enrolled in day care three times a week.

The baby was delivered, and handed to the pediatrician, who breathed and cried immediately.

After the tea break, staff should empty the teapot and stand upside down on the draining board.

3-year-old teacher needed for pre-school

Mixing bowl set designed to please a cook with round bottom for efficient beating

Killer Sentenced to Die for Second Time in 10 Years

Two Sisters Reunited After 18 Years in Checkout Counter

Local High School Dropouts Cut in Half

Include your children when baking cookies.

Wanted: Man to take care of cow that does not smoke or drink

Coming home, I drove into the wrong house and collided with a tree I don't have.

I was thrown from the car as it left the road. I was later found in the ditch by some stray cows.

Materials needed: lists of bloopers, paper and markers

Misplaced and Left Dangling in Room 220

As you find dangling participles and misplaced modifiers in your students' writing, pause to laugh about it. After all, laughing at oneself is quite acceptable these days, thanks to TV's blooper shows, sitcom outtakes, and funny home videos catching the famous and not-so-famous in the act of being human. Create a class book that can grow from year to year, titled something like *Misplaced and Left Dangling in Room [your room number]*. When your students exhibit these anomalies in their writing, invite them to add a page to the class book. On the top half of the page, they write, "I wrote _____," and illustrate it. On the bottom half, they write and illustrate "But, I *really* meant to write _____."

Materials needed: paper, markers or crayons, materials for making a class book, students' writing

Check It Out!

Read the following student-written script, then answer the questions.

OLIVIA, 9, watches her MOTHER brush her hair in the mirror.

    OLIVIA

1. Whose hair do I have?

    MOTHER

2. You have your grandmother's beautiful hair.

    OLIVIA

3. Whose nose do I have?

    MOTHER

4. You have your father's wonderful nose.

    OLIVIA

5. Whose smile do I have?

6. Her mother turns to face her child and gives a wide grin. She is beautiful.

    MOTHER

7. You have my smile.

8. Olivia smiles. This makes her very happy.

Use these terms to answer the following questions:

posessive noun
possessive pronoun
verb
adjective
adverb
preposition
coordinating conjunction
interjection

1. In line 1, *whose* is a _____.

2. In line 2, *grandmother's* is a _____.

3. In line 3, *do* is a _____.

4. In line 4, *wonderful* is a _____.

5. In line 5, *have* is a _____.

6. In line 6, *and* is a _____.

7. In line 7, *my* is a _____.

8. In line 8, *very* is a _____.

Final Thoughts: A Spoonful of Sugar

Parents know that even the worst pills are palatable when mixed in sugar, applesauce, or peanut butter. It's no accident that pharmaceutical companies make children's medicine in orange, grape, and cherry flavors. Adults know that children will approach that which tastes good and run from that which does not.

Unfortunately, grammar often is treated like a bitter pill that tastes more like castor oil or chalk. We approach it with an attitude of "Here, let me hold you down and force this down your throat—I don't like this any more than you do—trust me, it hurts me more than it hurts you—be patient—this will be over soon." As a result, children run from it, remembering it with disdain if they remember it at all. We forget about the spoonful of sugar.

This book has given you ideas for sweetening grammar study in your classroom. We hope you have had a good time playing with grammar, that you are feeling more confident about your own understanding, and that you have a heightened sensitivity to the challenges English grammar poses for English language learners. Most of all, we hope that you have a new resolve to make grammar a lively and joyous part of your classroom study. We have a wonderful language that opens others' thoughts to us and our thoughts to others, so let's continue to share. We wish you happy and playful parsing!

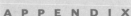

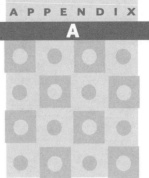

Grades at Which Grammatical Concepts Commonly Are Taught

	1	2	3	4	5	6	7	8
NOUNS								
Singular/Plural	●	●	●	●	●	●	●	●
Common/Proper	●	●	●	●	●	●	●	●
Possessives		●	●	●	●	●	●	●
VERBS								
Action	●	●	●	●	●	●	●	●
Transitive/Intransitive						●	●	●
Being	●	●	●	●	●	●	●	●
Helping			●	●	●	●	●	●
Linking			●	●	●	●	●	●
Verbals								
Infinitives							●	●
Gerunds								●
Participles							●	●
Regular Verbs								
Present Tense Singular/Plural	●	●	●	●	●	●	●	●
Past Tense Singular/Plural	●	●	●	●	●	●	●	●
Future Tense Singular/Plural			●	●	●	●	●	●
Irregular Verbs		●	●	●	●	●	●	●
Tenses								
Simple Tense				●	●	●	●	●
Perfect Tense					●	●	●	●
Progressive Tense							●	●
Perfect Progressive Tense								●
Direct/Indirect Objects					●	●	●	●
Subject-Verb Agreement					●	●	●	●
PRONOUNS								
Singular and Plural					●	●	●	●
Cases								
Subjective (Nominative)			●	●	●	●	●	●

	1	2	3	4	5	6	7	8
PRONOUNS (*cont.*)								
Cases (*cont.*)								
Objective			●	●	●	●	●	●
Possessive			●	●	●	●	●	●
Pronoun-Antecedent Agreement					●	●	●	●
ADJECTIVES								
Positive, Comparative, Superlative	●	●	●	●	●	●	●	●
Functions								
Descriptive	●	●	●	●	●	●	●	●
Limiting								
Possessive						●	●	●
Demonstrative						●	●	●
Indefinite						●	●	●
Interrogative						●	●	●
Numerical					●	●	●	●
Articles		●	●	●	●	●	●	●
ADVERBS			●	●	●	●	●	●
Comparative, Superlative				●	●	●	●	●
CONJUNCTIONS								
Coordinating				●	●	●	●	●
Subordinating							●	●
Correlative								●
INTERJECTIONS						●	●	●
PREPOSITIONS				●	●	●	●	●
SUBJECT AND PREDICATE	●	●	●	●	●	●	●	●
TYPES OF SENTENCES								
Simple				●	●	●	●	●
Compound				●	●	●	●	●
Complex						●	●	●
Compound-Complex								●
FUNCTIONS								
Declarative	●	●	●	●	●	●	●	●
Interrogative	●	●	●	●	●	●	●	●
Exclamatory	●	●	●	●	●	●	●	●
CLAUSES								
Independent						●	●	●
Dependent						●	●	●
PHRASES								
Prepositional Phrases				●	●	●	●	●
Infinitive Phrases							●	●
Gerund Phrases								●

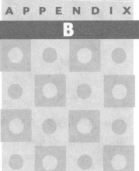
Test Yourself

Use the following sentence for items 1–8.

New teachers should have a working knowledge of grammar and usage.

1. The complete subject of this sentence is

    A teachers   **C** new teachers should have

    B new teachers   **D** teachers . . . have

2. The complete predicate of this sentence is

    A should   **C** should have a working knowledge

    B should have   **D** should have a working knowledge of
                         grammar and usage.

3. The sentence is a _____ sentence.

    A simple   **C** complex

    B compound   **D** compound-complex

4. *working* is

    A an adjective   **C** an adverb

    B a verb   **D** a noun

5. This sentence is

    A declarative   **C** imperative

    B interrogative   **D** exclamatory

6. There are _____ common nouns in this sentence.

    A 1   **C** 3

    B 2   **D** 4

7. *should* is a

    A helping verb   **B** linking verb

117

8. a working knowledge is

   A a direct object   **C** an adverbial

   B an indirect object   **D** a prepositional phrase

Use the following sentence to answer items 9–16

While today's university seniors report that they were not taught grammar formally, they will be required to teach it to their future students.

9. This sentence is a _____ sentence.

   A simple   **C** compound

   B complex   **D** compound-complex

10. *While today's university seniors report that they were not taught grammar formally* is

   A an independent clause   **B** a dependent clause

11. *they will be required to teach it to their future students* is

   A an independent clause   **B** a dependent clause

12. In *to teach it*, *it* refers to

   A teach   **C** grammar

   B they   **D** students

13. *formally* is

   A an adjective   **C** a preposition

   B an adverb   **D** a noun

14. *to teach* is

   A a prepositional phrase **C** a gerund

   B an infinitive   **D** a dependent clause

15. *they will be required* contains

   A a personal pronoun   **C** future tense

   B an auxiliary verb   **D** all of the above

16. There are _____ adjectives in this sentence.

   A 1   **C** 3

   B 2   **D** 4

Use the following sentence for items 17–22.

When Rifka gave Ed the recipe, the other family members were overcome with joy.

17. *Rifka* is

    A a direct object   **C** a proper noun

    B a common noun   **D** an indirect object

18. *Ed* is

    A a subject   **C** a direct object

    B an indirect object   **D** a verbal

19. The sentence is

    A simple   **C** compound

    B complex   **D** compound-complex

20. *gave* is

    A a transitive verb   **C** a verb of being

    B an intransitive verb   **D** a gerund

21. This sentence is an example of

    A correct subject-verb agreement

    B incorrect subject-verb agreement

22. This sentence is written in

    A present tense   **C** past tense

    B present perfect tense   **D** past perfect tense

Choose from the following for items 23–27.

    A who   **C** whoever

    B whom   **D** whomever

23. To _____ can the student appeal for support?

24. _____ comes in first will receive the trophy.

25. _____ decided to study together?

26. The professor should inform _____ she sees.

27. With _____ did Kevin study?

Choose from the following for items 28–30.

    A Whose   **B** Who's

28. _____ book is this?

29. _____ that at the door?

30. _____ afraid of the big bad wolf?

Identify the type of adjective that is underlined in sentences 31–34.

    A possessive   **C** indefinite

    B demonstrative   **D** interrogative

____**31.** You may play <u>either</u> song.

____**32.** <u>This</u> mouse belongs with Luis' computer.

____**33.** <u>My</u> students grew to love grammar.

____**34.** <u>Whose</u> pencil did I take?

35. What is the _____ of books that we need to order?

    A amount   **B** number

36. What do you think will be the _____ of testing the students in each grade?

    A affect   **B** effect

37. _____ mother called to say that there is a family emergency.

    A You're   **B** Your

38. Are the students _____ for the final exam?

    A all ready   **B** already

39. The _____ judge decided the case in a fair way.

    A uninterested   **B** disinterested

40. _____ the book on Mike's desk when you are finished with it.

    A Lie   **B** Lay

41. We were _____ by 5:00 p.m..

    A already   **B** all ready

42. The exam was harder _____ we thought it would be.

    A then   **B** than

43. Maya didn't state it for certain, but she _____ that she would be going to the ballet.

    A implied   **B** inferred

44. The bachelor walked _____ the three bachelorettes.

    A between   **B** among

45. Jane looked _____ even though she had recently been ill.

    A good   **B** well

46. In the sentence "*She gave him her report*," the cases of the three pronouns, *in order*, are

    A nominative, possessive, objective

    B possessive, nominative, objective

    C nominative, objective, possessive

    D none of the above

Answer questions 47–50 using the following choices.

    A incorrect positive/comparative/superlative

    B dangling participle

    C wrong pronoun case

    D lacks subject-verb agreement

___**47.** Each of the students in the class have a unique assignment.

___**48.** Us Philadelphians know all about soft pretzels and water ice.

___**49.** Scoring the highest on the exam, the prize seemed a given.

___**50.** Lesley earned the highest score of the two of them.

Identify the underlined word in order to answer questions 51–55.

    A coordinating conjunction

    B subordinating conjunction

    C correlative conjunction

___**51.** David eats tomatoes _even though_ he is allergic to them.

___**52.** _Neither_ Bette _nor_ Heshie lives in Pennsylvania.

___**53.** Lou _and_ Dora were married almost fifty years.

___**54.** _Not only_ is Dr. Loft brilliant _but_ she _also_ is creative.

___**55.** _Although_ Helena lives far away, she visits Katy often.

Use the following story to answer questions 56–75. The sentences are numbered so that you can find them easily when answering the questions.

1. _There were three pigs named Alfonzo Pigg, Benjamin Pigg, and Cassius Pigg_. 2. _Their_ mother, Mrs. Michelle Pigg, told them to go out into the world so they could be on their own. 3. Mrs. Pigg _wanted_ to prepare them for adulthood. 4. Alfonzo met a farmer who was trudging along _with a load of straw_. 5. He asked _the man_ for some of his straw and the kind farmer answered, "Sure." 6. So Alfonzo took the straw and built _himself_ a lovely ranch. 7. Benjamin Pigg _was_ lucky enough to see a carpenter carrying a load of sticks. 8. He begged the carpenter for some of his sticks and the clueless carpenter was kind _enough_ to give him some. 9. Benjamin took the sticks and built himself a _lovely_ chalet. 10. Cassius Pigg was the _luckier_ of the three. 11. He met a _construction_ worker driving a dump truck full of bricks. 12. He asked for _some_ bricks and the construction worker gave him enough to build himself a beautiful piggy mansion. 13. In the same town, Mr. B. B. Wolf struck terror in pigs' _hearts_. 14. _Walking_ is such good exercise, he thought as he ambled along, when suddenly he saw the lovely domicile of straw. 15. He bellowed to Alfonzo, "_Mr. Pigg, Mr. Pigg, let me in!_" 16. _Well_, the frightened Alfonzo stuttered, "No way," and BB subsequently huffed and puffed and blew the house down. 17. Alfonzo escaped to his brother's house made of sticks, and BB set out _hungrily_ to look for the rest of the Pigg brothers' homes. 18. _As you probably have guessed, BB blew down the stick chalet, then he moved on to try his luck at blowing down the brick piggy mansion_. 19. When BB couldn't blow the brick house _down_, he decided to climb down the chimney. 20. When he reached the bottom of the chimney, he landed in a pot of boiling water and cried out, "I _should have known_ these Pigg brothers would try to turn me into wolf stew!"

56. The first sentence is

    A simple   **C** complex

    B compound   **D** compound-complex

57. *Their* in sentence 2 is

    A a subjective pronoun   **C** a possessive pronoun

    B an objective pronoun   **D** none of the above

58. In sentence 3, *wanted* is

    A present tense   **C** past perfect tense

    B past tense   **D** future tense

59. In sentence 4, *with a load of straw* is

    A an independent clause   **C** a prepositional phrase

    B a verbal   **D** an adverbial phrase

60. In sentence 5, *the man* is

    A a direct object

    B an object of a preposition

    C an indirect object

    D a proper noun

61. In sentence 6, *himself* is

    A a demonstrative pronoun

    B an indefinite pronoun

    C a reciprocal pronoun

    D a reflexive pronoun

62. In sentence 7, *was* is

    A a transitive verb   **C** a helping verb

    B an intransitive verb   **D** a copulative verb

63. In sentence 8, *enough* is

    A a noun   **C** an adjective

    B an adverb   **D** a verb

64. In sentence 9, *lovely* is

    A a noun   **C** an adjective

    B an adverb   **D** a verb

65. In sentence 10, the use of *luckier* is

   A correct   **B** incorrect

66. In sentence 11, *construction* is

   A a demonstrative adjective

   B a descriptive adjective

   C a possessive adjective

   D an indefinite adjective

67. In sentence 12, *some* is

   A a demonstrative adjective

   B a possessive adjective

   C an indefinite adjective

   D an interrogative adjective

68. In sentence 13, *hearts* is

   A the object of a preposition

   B a plural noun

   C part of an independent clause

   D all of the above

69. In sentence 14, *walking* is

   A an adverb   **C** an infinitive

   B a gerund   **D** all of the above

70. In sentence 15, *Mr. Pigg, Mr. Pigg, let me in!* is

   A declarative   **C** imperative

   B interrogative   **D** exclamatory

71. In sentence 16, *Well* is

   A an adjective   **C** an interjection

   B an adverb   **D** a noun

72. In sentence 17, *hungrily* is

   A an adjective   **C** a noun

   B an adverb   **D** a verb

73. Sentence 18 is

   A simple   **C** complex

   B compound   **D** compound-complex

74. In sentence 19, *down* is

    A a noun   **C** an adjective

    B a verb   **D** an adverb

75. In sentence 20, *should have known* is

    A simple tense   **C** progressive tense

    B perfect tense   **D** perfect progressive tense

ANSWERS

1. B	16. D	31. C	46. C	61. D
2. D	17. C	32. B	47. D	62. D
3. A	18. B	33. A	48. C	63. B
4. A	19. B	34. D	49. B	64. C
5. A	20. A	35. B	50. A	65. B
6. D	21. A	36. B	51. B	66. B
7. A	22. C	37. B	52. C	67. C
8. A	23. B	38. A	53. A	68. D
9. B	24. C	39. B	54. C	69. B
10. B	25. A	40. B	55. B	70. C
11. A	26. D	41. B	56. A	71. C
12. C	27. B	42. B	57. C	72. B
13. B	28. A	43. A	58. B	73. D
14. B	29. B	44. B	59. C	74. D
15. D	30. B	45. B	60. C	75. D

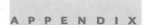

A Collection of Collective Nouns

agenda (tasks)

armada (ships)

army (ants)

band (gorillas, blue jays)

bank (monitors)

barren (mules)

bed (clams, oysters)

bevy (quail, swans)

blessing (unicorns)

bouquet (pheasants)

brigade (soldiers)

cast (actors, characters, falcons)

chain (islands)

charm (finches)

chorus (angels, singers)

cloud (gnats)

cluster (grasshoppers)

colony (ants, bats, beavers)

congregation (worshippers)

congress (baboons)

covey (grouse, pheasants)

descent (woodpeckers)

division (soldiers)

down (hares)

dray (squirrels)

drove (cattle)

exaltation (larks)

fleet (ships)

flight (doves)

flock (birds, sheep, tourists)

gaggle (geese)

galaxy (stars, starlets)

gam (whales)

grist (bees)

herd (elephants)

hill (beans)

host (angels, sparrows)

huddle (lawyers)

leap (leopards)

leash (foxes)

litter (kittens, puppies)

mob (kangaroos)

muster (peacocks, storks)

network (computers)

nye (pheasants)

parliament (owls)

plague (locusts)

platoon (soldiers)

pod (seals, dolphins)

pride (lions)

range (mountains)

ring (keys)

school (fish)

sedge (cranes)

slither (snakes)

stand (trees)

swarm (bees, rats)

team (athletes, ducks, horses)

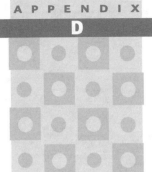
Jean's Suggested Music for Rachmaninoff to Reggae to Rap

Beethoven's Symphony no. 5 (last thirty seconds of third movement, going into fourth)

"Born to Run"—Bruce Springsteen

"Live Like You Were Dying"—Tim McGraw

Afternoon of a Faun—Claude Debussey

"The Wreck of the Edmund Fitzgerald"—Gordon Lightfoot

In the Hall of the Mountain King—Edvard Grieg

"God Bless America"—Irving Berlin

The Phantom of the Opera—Andrew Lloyd Webber

"God Bless the USA (. . . and I'm proud to be an American)"—Lee Greenwood

New World Symphony, movement 2—Antonin Dvorak

The Moldau—Bedrich Smetana

The 4th of July—Charles Ives

The Washington Post March—John Phillip Sousa

"I Walk the Line"—Johnny Cash

Opus 10. Air (Dublinesque)—Billy Joel (from his classical CD)

"I Can't Stand the Rain"—Tina Turner

"O Fortuna" (from *Carmina Burana*)—Carl Orff

"Take the 'A' Train"—Duke Ellington

"Strange Fruit"—Billie Holiday

"Baker Street" (intro)—Gerry Rafferty

Sabre Dance—Aram Khachaturian

Adagio for Strings—Samuel Barber

"Brain Damage" (from *Dark Side of the Moon*)—Pink Floyd

"The Day Begins" (from *Days of Future Past*)—Moody Blues

"Sleigh Ride"—Meredith Wilson

William Tell Overture—Gioacchino Antonio Rossini

Pomp and Circumstance nos. 1 and 4—Edward Elgar

"I Will Survive"—Gloria Gaynor

Overture to *Messiah*—G. F. Handel

any fugue by J. S. Bach

any rap by Eminem (check for language)

anything by Metallica (check for language)

List developed by N. Jean Bender, music teacher, Oxford Area High School, Oxford, Pennsylvania.

Additional Resources for Classroom Use

Caudle, Brad, and Richard Caudle. 1994. *Rock 'n Learn Grammar*. Conroe, TX: Rock 'n Learn.

Chanko, Pamela. 2004. *Grammar Tales: Teaching Guide*. New York: Scholastic.

Egan, Lorraine Hopping. 2001. *Noun Hounds and Other Great Grammar Games*. New York: Scholastic.

Greenberg, Dan. 2000. *Comic-Strip Grammar*. New York: Scholastic.

Katz, Bobbi. 1999. *25 Great Grammar Poems with Activities*. New York: Scholastic.

Kellahar, Karen. 2000. *Grammar Puzzles and Games Kids Can't Resist*. New York: Scholastic.

Larson, Randy. 2003. *Hot Fudge Monday: Tasty Ways to Teach Parts of Speech to Students Who Have a Hard Time Swallowing Anything to Do with Grammar*. Fort Collins, CO: Cottonwood.

Mack, Nancy. 2005. *Teaching Grammar with Playful Poems*. New York: Scholastic.

Pulver, Robin. 2003. *Punctuation Takes a Vacation*. New York: Holiday House.

Sanders, Nancy I. 2004. *Grammar Manipulatives Kids Love!* New York: Scholastic.

Sunley, Laura. 2002. *Fun with Grammar*. New York: Scholastic.

Van Zile, Susan. 2003. *Awesome Hands-on Activities for Teaching Grammar*. New York: Scholastic.

APPENDIX
F

Check It Out! Test Answers

Chapter 2 Answers

1. b 5. c
2. c 6. a
3. a 7. b
4. d 8. d

Chapter 3 Answers

proper noun, singular (common) noun, proper nouns (3), collective noun, plural noun

1. subjective, possessive
2. subjective, possessive
3. subjective, subjective
4. demonstrative, possessive
5. subjective, subjective, demonstrative
6. subjective, objective, objective, subjective
7. interrogative, demonstrative
8. indefinite, objective
9. reflexive, objective, subjective, subjective

Chapter 4 Answers

1. verb of being, present; verb of being, present perfect
2. verb of being, present; action verb, past
3. action verb, present perfect
4. being/action verb, present progressive
5. verb of being, present
6. action verb, present
7. verb of being, present
8. action verb, present perfect progressive; action verb, future
9. verb of being, future perfect progressive; being verb, future; action verb, past

Chapter 5 Answers

1. descriptive
2. indefinite; numerical
3. descriptive
4. possessive; numerical; descriptive
5. demonstrative; article
6. superlative

130

The Revolutionary War Answers

1. anew
2. strongly
3. around that . . .
4. loudly, silently

Chapter 6 Answers

1. and (coordinating conjunction)
2. of (preposition); and (coordinating conjunction)
3. from (preposition); in (preposition); about (preposition)
4. and (coordinating conjunction); until (preposition)
5. to (preposition); with (preposition); until (preposition)
6. although (subordinating conjunction); and (coordinating conjunction)
7. to (preposition); although (subordinating conjunction); or (preposition); of (preposition); from (preposition); and (coordinating conjunction); of (preposition)
8. to (preposition); with (preposition); of (preposition)
9. both/and (correlative conjunctions)
10. Oh! (strong interjection); of (preposition)

Chapter 7 Answers

1. possessive pronoun
2. possessive noun
3. verb
4. adjective
5. verb
6. coordinating conjunction
7. possessive pronoun
8. adverb

Works Cited

Barton, Byron. 1993. *The Little Red Hen*. New York: Harper Collins.

Bladon, Rachel. 2000. *Improve Your Grammar*. London: Usborne.

Braddock, Richard, Richard Lloyd-Jones, and Lowell Schoer. 1963. *Research in Written Composition*. Champaign, IL: National Council of Teachers of English.

Brandon, Lee. 2006. *Sentences at a Glance*. 3d ed. Boston: Houghton Mifflin.

Bouchard, David. 1995. *If You're Not from the Prairie*. New York: Atheneum.

Brown, Alvin. 1996. "Correct Grammar So Essential to Effective Writing Can Be Taught—Really!" *English Journal* 85 (7): 98–101.

Bunting, Eve. 1996. *Secret Place*. New York: Clarion.

Burleigh, Robert. 1998. *Home Run*. San Diego: Harcourt Brace.

Cadnum, Michael. 1997. *The Lost and Found House*. New York: Viking.

Carle, Eric. 1984. *The Very Busy Spider*. New York: Putnam.

Carroll, Lewis. 1872. *Through the Looking-Glass and What Alice Found There*. London: Macmillan.

Cazort, Douglas. 1997. *Under the Grammar Hammer*. Los Angeles: Lowell House.

Child, Lydia Maria. 1884. *Flowers for Children*. Vol. 2. Boston: J. H. Francis.

Conford, Ellen. 1980. *The Revenge of the Incredible Dr. Rancid and His Youthful Assistant, Jeffrey*. New York: Scholastic.

Daily Oral Language K–12. 1993. Wilmington, MA: Great Source Education Group.

Ehrenworth, Mary, and Vicki Vinton. 2005. *The Power of Grammar: Unconventional Approaches to the Conventions of Language*. Portsmouth, NH: Heinemann.

Ellsworth, Blanche, and John Higgins. 2004. *English simplified*. 10th ed. New York: Pearson/Longman.

Fox, Mem. 1986. *Hattie and the Fox*. New York: Aladdin Paperbacks USA.

Freeman, David, and Yvonne Freeman. 2004. *Essential Linguistics: What You Need to Know to Teach*. Portsmouth, NH: Heinemann.

Fries, Charles. 1952. *The Structure of English: An Introduction to the Construction of English Sentences*. New York: Harcourt Brace.

Galdone, Paul. 1981. *The Three Billy Goats Gruff*. New York: Clarion.

———. 1984. *Henny Penny*. New York: Clarion.

Gardner, Howard. 1993. *Frames of Mind: The Theory of Multiple Intelligences*. New York: Harper Collins.

Goldstein, Barbara, Jack Waugh, and Karen Linsky. 2004. *Grammar to Go: How It Works and How to Use It*. Boston: Houghton Mifflin.

Gray, Libba Moore. 1995. *My Mama Had a Dancing Heart*. New York: Orchard.

Gutman, Anne, and Georg Hallensleben. 2003. *Mommy Hugs*. San Francisco: Chronicle.

Haussamen, Brock. 2000. *Revising the Rules*. Dubuque, IA: Kendall/Hunt.

———. 2003. *Grammar Alive! A Guide for Teachers*. Urbana, IL: National Council of Teachers of English.

Herron, Carolivia. 1997. *Nappy Hair*. New York: Knopf.

Hillocks, George Jr., and Michael Smith. 1991. "Grammar and Usage." In *Handbook of Research on Teaching the English Language Arts*, edited by James Flood. New York: Macmillan.

Hoffman, Sandra Josephs, and Donna Hooker Topping. 1999. "Changing the Face of Teaching and Learning Through Teacher-Research." In *Creative Teaching—Act 2*, edited by Hans Kline. 173–82. Madison, WI: Omni.

———. 2000. "Neglected Voices: What Case Method Research Can Tell Us About the Stakeholders in Education." In *Complex Demands on Teaching Require Innovation: Case Method and Other Techniques*, edited by Hans Klein. 49–54. Madison, WI: Omni.

Hunter, Anthony. 1996. "A New Grammar That Has Clearly Improved Writing." *English Journal* (November): 102–7.

Hutchins, Pat. 1971. *Rosie's Walk*. New York: Aladdin.

Invernizzi, Marcia, Mary Abouzeid, and Janet Bloodgood. 1997. "Integrated Word Study: Spelling, Grammar, and Meaning in the Language Arts Classroom." *Language Arts* 74: 185–92.

Jessup, Harley. 1997. *What's Alice Up To?* New York: Viking.

Kiester, Jane Bell. 1993. *Caught'ya Again! More Grammar with a Giggle*. Gainesville, FL: Maupin House.

Kolln, Martha, and Robert Funk. 2002. *Understanding English Grammar*. 6th ed. New York: Longman.

Lewis, Jone Johnson. 2005. "Over the River and Through the Wood: The Woman Who Wrote the Winter Favorite." *www.womenhistory.about.com/od/child lydiamaria/a/over_the_river.htm*

Loberger, Gordon, and Kate Welsh. 2002. *Webster's New World English Grammar Handbook*. Indianapolis: Wiley.

Lortie, Dan. 1975. *Schoolteacher*. Chicago: University of Chicago Press.

Lowry, Lois. 1990. *Number the Stars*. New York: Dell.

MacLachlan, Patricia. 1995. *What You Know First*. New York: Harper Collins.

Martinsen, Amy. 2000. "The Tower of Babel and the Teaching of Grammar: Writing Instruction for a New Century." *English Journal* (September): 122–26.

Meyer, Franklyn. 1969. *Me and Caleb Again*. River Grove, IL: Follett.

Mulroy, David. 2003. *The War Against Grammar*. Portsmouth, NH: Heinemann.

Neufeldt, Victoria, and David Guralnik, eds. *Webster's New World Dictionary of American English*. New York: Webster's New World.

Ray, Katie Wood. 1999. *Wondrous Words*. Urbana/Champaign, IL: National Council of Teachers of English.

Reed, Alonzo, and Brainerd Kellogg. 1987. *Higher Lessons in English (1886)*. Ann Arbor, MI: Scholars' Facsimiles and Reprints.

Rowling, J. K. 2000. *Harry Potter and the Goblet of Fire*. New York: Scholastic.

Rylant, Cynthia. 1982. *When I Was Young in the Mountains*. New York: Dutton.

———. 1985a. *The Relatives Came*. Scarsdale, NY: Bradbury.

———. 1985b. *The Whales*. New York: Scholastic.

———. 1992. *Missing May*. New York: Orchard.

Safire, William. 1990. *Fumblerules: A Lighthearted Guide to Grammar and Good Usage*. New York: Dell.

Sams, Lynn. 2003. "How to Teach Grammar, Analytical Thinking, and Writing: A Method That Works." *English Journal* (January): 57–65.

Schuster, Edgar. 2003. *Breaking the Rules: Liberating Writers Through Innovative Grammar Instruction*. Portsmouth, NH: Heinemann.

Spinelli, Jerry. 1990. *Maniac Magee: A Novel*. Boston: Little, Brown.

Steinberg, Laya. 2003. *Thesaurus Rex*. Cambridge, MA: Barefoot.

Swan, Michael, and Bernard Smith. 2001. *Learner English*, 2nd ed. Cambridge: Cambridge University Press.

Swartz, E. 2003. "Skill Activities for Levels Pre-K–8." *Teaching PreK–8* (January): 70.

Taback, Simms. 2002. *This Is the House That Jack Built*. New York: G. P. Putnam and Sons.

Topping, Donna H., and Sandra J. Hoffman. 2003. "After Teacher-Research, Then What?" *Ohio Journal of the English Language Arts* 43 (2): 30–37.

Topping, Donna Hooker, and Roberta Ann McManus. 2002a. "A Culture of Literacy in Science." *Educational Leadership* 60 (November): 30–33.

———. 2002b. *Real Reading, Real Writing: Content Area Strategies*. Portsmouth, NH: Heinemann.

Van Zile, Susan. 2003. "Grammar That'll Move You." *Instructor* (January): 32–4.

Viorst, Judith. 1987. *Alexander and the Terrible, Horrible, No Good, Very Bad Day*. New York: Atheneum.

Warburton, Tom, dir. 1973/1997. *Schoolhouse Rock! Grammar Rock*. Los Angeles: Disney Studios.

Ward, Lynd. 1952. *The Biggest Bear*. New York: Houghton Mifflin.

Weaver, Constance. 1996. "Teaching Grammar in the Context of Writing," *English Journal* (November): 15–24.

White, E. B. 1970. *The Trumpet of the Swan*. New York: Harper Trophy.

———. 1974. *Stuart Little*. New York: Harper Trophy.

Wood, Audrey. 1984. *The Napping House*. New York: Harcourt.

Yolen, Jane. 1992. *Letting Swift River Go*. Boston: Little, Brown.

———. 1993. *Welcome to the Green House*. New York: Putnam.

———. 1997. *Miz Berlin Walks*. New York: Putnam.